ADVANCE PRAISE

"In 'Freefall,' Cindy Kaplan chronicles her evolution as a mother as she undertakes her own journey toward self-acceptance. Along the way, she offers an invitation to open our hearts to our children and to ourselves."
—**Tova Mirvis, bestselling author of "The Book of Separation"**

"'Freefall' is the story of a beautiful journey of a mother of three children and her learnings while attempting to 'fix' one of them who has special needs."
—**Sonia Sumar, founder of Yoga for the Special Child**

"In her memoir, 'Freefall,' Cindy tells her story in a captivating way, while simultaneously providing insight, meaning, healing and hope. This book is not just for parents with differently abled children, it is for all parents seeking transformati
—**Suzi Lula, bestselling author of "The M Evolution: How Thriving Mothers Raise Children"**

"'Freefall' is a book every parent should read. Not just parents who've endured impossible loss or uncertainty, but those who have experienced the space between their expectations and the truth of who their child is or will become."
—Justine Wiltshire Cohen, director and principal of Down Under Yoga

"A sensitive and powerful book that will speak lovingly to all parents, regardless of their circumstances."
—Jacky Davis, New York Times bestselling author of "Ladybug Girl" series

freefall

*One Mother's Journey Raising a
Child With Special Needs*

CINDY KAPLAN

PUBLISH **HER**

FREEFALL: ONE MOTHER'S JOURNEY RAISING A CHILD
WITH SPECIAL NEEDS

© Copyright 2022 Cindy Kaplan

This book is memoir. It reflects the author's present recollections of experiences over
time. Some names and characteristics may have been changed, some events may
have been compressed, and some dialogue may have been recreated.

Company and/or product names referenced in this book may be logos, trade names,
trademarks, and/or registered trademarks, and are the property of their respective
owners.

ISBN: 979-8-9850242-8-9
Printed in the United States of America
First Printing: 2022

Published by Publish Her, LLC
2909 South Wayzata Boulevard
Minneapolis, MN 55405
www.publishherpress.com

Cover design by Kayla Franz

Cover photo by Krista Guenin, Krista Photography
www.kristaphoto.com

To my mother and Mira,
whose gifts shine the light on our souls

FOREWORD

"My daughter, Mira, cannot walk nor live independently. She suffered a brain injury during labor and delivery."

Cindy's words reverberated deep within my soul. I couldn't hold back my emotions. I asked her to tell me her story. As she did, I was awestruck. I urged her to write it down and share it. It was too compelling to go unheard. "Freefall: One Mother's Journey to Raising a Child With Special Needs" is the outcome of that conversation.

When Mira entered the world, Cindy's expectations of her daughter and her visions of motherhood were shattered. Most of us are not prepared for parenthood on the best day. Cindy had not imagined spending the first month of Mira's life by her side in the hospital rather than at home. She immediately stepped into her patterned role of being the ultimate rescuer and savior. She went into overdrive to compensate for her precious daughter's possible brokenness.

Over time, Cindy began to lose her sense of self. She noticed she was not joyful or playful in the way she knew herself to be. It was then that Cindy realized she needed to change her life and start living in a way that was in stark contrast to the way she had been. This is exactly what she did.

"Freefall" is the story of Cindy's journey of rebirth and transformation. The pages of this book are filled with the bravery of one mother's journey raising a child with special needs. It is a story for every parent, and it is also for every human who needs to reconcile with the hand they were dealt, which Cindy has done with beauty and grace.

I know this story will touch you the way it did me. More so, it will grow and inspire you to become an even better parent and person than you already are. This is what stories do—they elevate and evolve us.

While this book is a personal memoir, it is much more. It is an ode to the power of parental love and the resilience of each child's spirit. Most of all, it is a testament to the unshakable bond between mother and daughter. It will teach you how to live in the present, find gratitude in your life and discover insurmountable courage you never dreamed you had.

Dr. Shefali Tsabary
Clinical Psychologist
New York Times bestselling author of
"The Conscious Parent"

CHAPTER ONE:

MIRA ENTERS THE WORLD

"She needs a haircut," observed Noah, our 3-year-old.

We'd brought him to the neonatal intensive care unit to see our newborn daughter. There was a sink for hand-washing immediately upon entry to the NICU. I washed my hands first, and then Noah, without any fuss, washed his own. I reached for his hand, and we walked down the long hallway, passing nurses in blue scrubs and babies in incubators behind glass windows where only medical experts were allowed.

With each step closer to Mira, I imagined what it would be like for Noah to experience being a big brother. I felt my gut and throat tighten. What would he think of all the tubes, wires and monitors? Would he be scared?

His yellow pant legs swooshed as we proceeded wordlessly down that hallway to meet his newborn sister. Even on his tiptoes, Noah was too little to see the babies behind the glass, but he certainly heard the beeps and dings from the various monitors.

Marc, my husband, was waiting for us by Mira's crib. He lifted Noah up to see Mira lying on her tiny hospital mattress. I watched my son take her in. As he vocalized her need for a haircut, my heart softened, my eyes smiled, and I glanced over at Marc.

It was true that Mira had come into this world with lots of hair, streaked with the kind of brown and blonde highlights many women pay to have done at salons. In the midst of circumstances that otherwise lacked any sense of normalcy, Noah's observation was wonderfully normal. What I didn't know at the time was that normal is a construct, a projection of what we have been taught to expect when a child enters our lives.

There were tubes and wires all over Mira's body—a tiny tube in her nose and a thicker one taped on her mouth, colored wires that led from sparkling silver stickers on her chest to monitors overhead, and more wires that decorated the top of her full head of hair.

There were always one or two nurses standing by her clear plastic crib, glancing up at the monitors and adjusting the dials and buttons on the side. Less than 10 feet away on either side of Mira's crib were other babies in incubators and cribs with monitors like Mira's that lit up with neon lines and made beeping sounds that came with no predictability.

A couple of years later, when I brought Mira to Noah's kindergarten class, one of the children noticed that one of Mira's eyes was focused inward and asked Noah, "Does your sister have crossed eyes?"

"No, she just has special needs," Noah explained in his usual, accepting, matter-of-fact way. To him, his sister was a person like any other.

When we told Noah that we had decided, at the recommendation of her ophthalmologist, to get Mira corrective surgery that would prevent her eye from turning inward, he said, "Why? That's just a part of Mira. That's who she is."

At 5, Noah couldn't understand the greater reasons for the surgery. But he was connected to a deeper truth I still had to learn. The beautiful thing about Noah was how naturally he accepted his sister from the start. It took a long time for me to measure up to my son's acceptance of Mira. I was learning how hard it can be for parents to accept who their child is, whether it's a physical issue that stems from birth or a child's inclination, temperament or interest that is different from one's own.

A month before Mira was born, my husband, son and I left our house of two years in Madison, Wisconsin, to move into the house where Marc grew up in Cambridge, Massachusetts. As renovations to parts of the house were not yet complete, we stayed with Marc's aunt for the month prior to moving into the house. On the morning of our move-in date, I stopped to get doughnuts for the movers, electrician and other contractors who'd be there completing the work. I had learned the ritual of providing treats for movers from my parents, who had always done so during the numerous local moves our family made when I was growing up.

I sat on the front steps of our Cambridge home, observing the neighboring houses built in the late 1800s. I delighted in the full bloom of the trees, some with roots bursting through the red brick sidewalks. I watched neighbors pass by on foot with groceries, others attending to small front gardens, and I filled my mind with fantasies of our next chapter.

My phone rang, abruptly bringing me back to reality. It was Marc with news that an airplane had crashed into the twin towers. I shared this information with the electrician, who showed up right as the movers began unloading boxes from their truck. His face drained of color. He told me his wife was on the train from Boston to New York for work.

As I imagined what was going through his mind, I struggled to make decisions about where furniture and boxes should go. I had a strong urge to tell them, "I don't care where the couch goes. Drop it on the sidewalk. I'll deal with it later."

The initial excitement of the day was swiftly overshadowed by fear, disbelief, sudden vulnerability and uncertainty. I will always recall the stress of this day as a harbinger of the fear and confusion that was to come.

A month later, Marc, Noah and I were at our kitchen table eating takeout sushi when I felt my water break. My body began to tremble as a rush of heat pulled me from my seat. The noises in the house suddenly became a background garble.

I said nothing but immediately headed to the bathroom. One foot in front of the other led me to the closet-sized room near the front door. As I realized my pants were soaked with blood, my heart raced. My brain reached for every possible explanation to create a different story than the one that was unfolding. *Perhaps this is normal*, I told myself. I bled with my first pregnancy early on. Despite my attempts to create a hopeful narrative, deep down I knew something was terribly wrong.

Holding back the panic that was flooding my body, I returned to the kitchen, where Marc and Noah were still eating. "I think my water broke," I said with a flat tone. "But it's bloody. I think we should call the midwife."

My trembling fingers managed to dial the numbers. The midwife at the hospital said, "It's most likely your cervix ripening. Why don't you come in so we can be sure?" I had already been a red flag to the doctors because of a high bilirubin count, otherwise they may have told me to stay at home.

Marc phoned his brother and asked him to come to our house to stay with Noah while we went to the hospital. It was Saturday evening. If I hadn't gone into labor by Monday, the doctors had already planned to induce me. I assured myself that since we lived close to some of the best hospitals in the country, I would be well taken care of.

As Marc drove to the hospital, I held my feet up on the dashboard, hoping to keep the blood inside my body.

"I can't believe we're about to have our baby," I said, wanting so badly to feel the excitement of the moment. The disconnect between what I was saying and how I was feeling was jarring. I knew my words were mostly for Marc. There wasn't room for two of us to be in a state of panic. I hoped my words might course-correct us from a detour from the birth I had imagined.

At the hospital, my head was hijacked by fear. I needed to get to the desk and explain what was happening, but I struggled to get the words out.

Once I was admitted, my baby's heart rate dropped. I followed the midwife's instructions, rolling onto one side and then the other. They thought if they adjusted me, her heart rate might improve. It didn't. The doctor who supervised the midwives entered the room and announced that the baby was in distress. He said it would be best if they performed a C-section.

I held tightly to the belief that I would have another vaginal birth, just like my first. As they wheeled me into the operating room, my palms sweaty and lips trembling, I had to let go of my plan.

At other moments in my life when I was scared, I had been able to sit with the fear as I figured out my next steps, playing out in my head the various scenarios with every possible outcome. This time I didn't have that luxury. What was about to happen to my body and my baby was out of my control. I was scared, but I could still follow directions and believed everyone was on our side and rooting for a healthy birth.

Robyn the midwife reached for my hand and held it. With the warmth of her hand in mine, my racing thoughts were tempered. This single point of connection made me feel less alone. There was so much my hand wanted to tell hers. I couldn't find a way to speak words of gratitude but hoped the touch of my palm would convey the message. Finally, my breathing began to slow. The connection assured me that we would get through this.

Suddenly, as I felt a strong urge to push, I was asked to sign release forms. Why was I expected to complete paperwork during a medical emergency? It seemed totally absurd. I would learn later that I was signing forms giving the doctors permission to cut me open without numbing or pain medication. My baby was in distress, and the doctor believed there was not enough time to allow the numbing medication to take hold.

Because this was my second child, and the baby's head was in view, the doctor told me to push. My body did exactly what it needed to do. Two pushes later, Mira entered the world. I don't recall if she cried immediately, but I do remember the nurses scooping her up and placing her on my chest so I could welcome her. Her face was colorless but beautiful. The rest of her was wrapped in a blanket.

Surrounded by a sea of blue medical scrubs, my only focus was her body as it laid on mine for mere moments. I held on to her warmth and the image of her full lips. Then, concerned about the baby's loss of blood, the nurses whisked her away.

Her full head of hair imprinted on my memory. I wondered if it would be my only memory.

For the next three hours, Marc and I sat together mostly in silence, interrupted by occasional visits from the doctor and midwife. They delivered news that left us feeling more unsure than ever.

"We are giving your daughter a blood transfusion," the doctor informed us. "She lost a lot of blood during delivery, so we are doing our best and will let you know as soon as you can see her."

Mingled with our love for one another, and our concern for our newborn daughter, Marc and I exchanged glances of shock and fear.

Because I had also lost a lot of blood, the staff prepared me for a blood transfusion. The doctor checked on me every 20 minutes.

"Mira is the first four letters of miracle," Marc pointed out in between all the check-ins. It was the name we had chosen for our daughter before she was born. We held tightly to this thought as we waited for more news.

We soon learned that almost every organ in Mira's body was shutting down. She was swollen like a Buddha, her eyes just slits, her belly puffy and round. She was having seizures, which the doctors told us was a common reaction to a brain injury and that time would tell whether they'd continue or not. I felt so ungrounded not knowing the state of Mira's health.

I became desperate to move, to see Mira, to do something.

I found the energy to sit up in bed, while Marc alternated between sitting and pacing. This was the time I had anticipated holding Mira in my arms, feeling her body against mine. *She should be getting to know me, and I should be getting to know her,* I thought. Nothing about this scene was in our playbook.

While Marc could get up and walk out of the room, he felt just as captive as I did. We tamped down our urges to call our parents, siblings and friends. Everything was on hold. Time was standing still. It felt as if we'd been sucked into a tornado and spit out on foreign land.

I would come to think of these first moments of Mira's life as "the space between," a place where, unlike the rest of my life, there was simply no road map. Not knowing was the greatest torture. *At least if I knew where we were headed,* I thought, *I would know what needed to be done.*

I began to adapt to the reality that knowing what to expect wasn't an option. We would have to wait and see what long-term effects this early damage would have on our little girl.

* * *

Within hours of Mira's birth, my father boarded a flight to Boston; my mother planned to fly out a week later. Marc and I took turns clinging from ropes of shock and despair to ropes of hope and competence, and Dad's pending arrival allowed me to hold a tighter grip on the latter. We had a beautiful baby girl! Dad's visit was both to celebrate Mira's arrival and to spread his fatherly wings around our pain and fear. His deep love of caring for others earned him the title "Jewish Mother" in our family.

It was Dad who insisted my younger brother wear an undershirt during the winter and that my older sister Jane and I had hats on as we walked out the door for school. Whether he knew we took them off as soon as we turned the street corner, I don't know. But he did his job of making sure our heads were covered until he lost sight of us.

Due to frequent travel for work, Dad hadn't been around much when I was growing up. Whenever my siblings and I were sick enough to warrant staying home from school, we counted on Mom to be there for daily care and doctor appointments, and we counted on Dad to bring home a get-well gift, often in the form of a stuffed animal. Now he'd been making up for his lack of presence by being extremely present with his grandchildren. He could always be counted on when someone was in need. It was he who called to get the details about his grandkids' games or the latest on someone's illness.

In Dad's eyes, his grandchildren could do no wrong. He enjoyed hearing stories about them and taking them shopping to get a new favorite toy. He wanted only to bring them love and joy. This day was no exception. Dad arrived at the hospital within Mira's first 24 hours, freshly showered and looking professional in a button-down shirt and jacket with jeans. We explained the details of what we knew about Mira so far.

He listened and expressed excitement about having a new granddaughter. His presence reassured me.

Ever a planner, he inquired about what we wanted to eat for dinner. He chatted with the nurses and doctors when they entered my room, bringing a sense of lightness, offering gratitude to them, and asking what nearby restaurants they would recommend. As we accepted multiple phone calls from family members and close friends, both congratulating us and offering us their prayers and wishes for Mira's health, Dad ordered food—enough to feed us and all the nurses on the floor.

I leaned into the comfort of my father's confidence and appreciated the distraction of having him there. I clung to it along with the words of friends and family who kept telling me we were in the best possible hospital.

We received many calls from family and friends checking in. Dad took a call on his cell phone and handed it to me. It was Mike, his dear friend and partner at work.

"Hi Mike," I said. A brief moment passed before he responded.

"Hey Cindy, how are you?" Another pause.

My heart rose in my chest as tears began to stream down my face. I knew Mike, but not well. I don't know what it was about him asking the same three words others had asked me repeatedly over the last 24 hours that was evoking this reaction now. The care in his voice and the slowness of his question felt like plunging into a trust fall and being held until, in my own time, I was ready to get up. It wasn't the words but the way he asked them, and the way I received his question, that felt so different. He exuded a sense of truly wanting to hear, along with the ability to hold whatever came to his ears.

* * *

On day three, we learned that due to blood loss and lack of oxygen, our beautiful daughter likely had cerebral palsy—an umbrella term for a condition where the brain is unable to communicate effectively with muscles in the body. I thought back to one of my teachers in elementary school who wore one shoe with a built-up platform and walked with a limp. Would Mira be like that?

When the neurologist came to talk with us, his manner was starkly clinical, void of compassion. "What cerebral palsy will mean specifically for your daughter is largely unknown," he said.

This was all I heard before my imagination began to run wild. Would Mira have a limp? Would she be able to walk on her own? Or would she be in a wheelchair, head tilted to the side, mouth drooling? I was grateful for the support of the chair under me as the doctor's cold demeanor obliterated my connection with Mira, and thoughts of brokenness and fear replaced what had been visions of hope.

I began to notice that the doctor stood each time he came to speak with us. Adorned with medical devices draped over his white medical coat, he always stood at the front of a team of residents. And we were always sitting in chairs. I felt 2 feet tall, powerless in his presence, and some part of me felt like I had done something wrong. I was acutely aware of my hesitancy to stand up and demand a basic level of respect. Where was the empathy or some explanation as to why all these strangers were getting a peek into this emotional and frightening new experience of ours? Where was the acknowledgment of our shock? At the very least, could he sit down with us for just a few moments?

* * *

I spent the following month connected like an emotional umbilical cord to the neonatal intensive care unit. I often found myself thinking of a mother in Noah's preschool who had given birth to a son about the same time Mira came into my life. I imagined this mother with her healthy baby, cooing with delight as he attained the mini milestones, such as his first smile.

You give and you give for the first several weeks and then that day, around six weeks, when you get that first smile, it all becomes worth it. This was something I heard on many occasions. I remembered experiencing this exactly with Noah and found myself anxiously wondering when Mira would give us her first smile. When would I be able to say it was all worth it?

I knew how important it was for me to hold Mira, but the nurses in the NICU told me she was simply too fragile. I sat and stood by her side for several hours a day and tried to communicate my love for her through my eyes and my presence. But I struggled with my feelings for her. Here was my child, hooked up to tubes through her nose, down her throat and in her veins. This, along with the monitors and all their sounds, only reinforced my fears that my daughter was broken.

When I was away from the hospital, my image of Mira became distorted and frightening. The disconnection between the baby I had envisioned and the baby who'd come from and through me was jolting. A part of me wondered if I had the capacity to love a child who was so different from what I expected. Knots formed in my stomach from my ability to even question this. I kept these feelings in a locked box of shame deep inside.

When I was with Mira, I saw a full and complete child—my child. Mira's body was in perfect form, exactly as I had expected, and yet she had suffered a loss of oxygen to her brain during labor and delivery. I had no idea how her development would unfold, no idea what parenting her would be like.

In some ways, my experience was not so different from any other new mother's experience. We believe we know who our baby is, but these thoughts are often based on expectations and fantasies. In Mira's case, her unknowns seemed so extreme, so removed from anything I had imagined. In the face of this unpredictability, I was desperate to grab onto something solid, a branch to keep me from this sudden and shocking freefall.

Over time, the NICU became a cocoon, a place of comfort where I could put all things aside except for my focus on Mira. How was it that simply seeing her tiny face and body put to rest all the frightening images and scenarios that tortured me when I was away from her?

I began learning my role and who I was as her mother. I learned how to hold her and how to place the U-shaped pillow around her legs so that they didn't splay outward. Then, when I was away from her again, I was mystified as to who I was as her mother. I didn't know myself outside of the roles I was learning to play by her side.

I adapted to the back-and-forth visits to the hospital and the calls to the NICU nurses at 2 a.m. to check on Mira and find out if I needed to bring them more breast milk. I became accustomed to the frequent hand-washing. I always found the blue faux leather chair that I preferred when sitting by her side. I discovered that the family room, filled with light from the window overlooking the Boston skyline, was ideal for pumping breast milk or having a phone conversation. I gained confidence as I learned to care for Mira with guidance from the NICU nurses. I found comfort in the routine.

As I settled into that routine, I asked for two things. One was to hold Mira. I didn't know much about the neonatal intensive care unit or raising a child with special needs, but I knew, from the depths of my soul, that it was essential that

I hold my child. I also knew the healing power of music, so I requested a CD player and brought in several CDs for Mira to listen to while we were together. In particular, I wanted to play Debbie Friedman's version of "Mi Shebeirach," a Hebrew prayer for healing:

> May the source of strength
> Who blessed the ones before us
> Help us find the courage
> To make our lives a blessing
> And let us say, Amen
> Bless those in need of healing
> With r'fuah sh'lemah
> The renewal of body
> The renewal of spirit
> And let us say, Amen

I grew up listening to and singing songs by Debbie Friedman at Jewish summer camps and at our synagogue, and this particular song had a way of bringing my heart straight to Mira. It created an instantaneous sense of belonging for me, with warmth and support from memories. I played this song in hopes of soothing and healing Mira, while instinctively hoping to also soothe and heal myself.

As the days went by, Mira became more comfortable drinking breast milk from me. One of the resident doctors told me he was surprised—he never imagined she would be able to breastfeed. I felt great pride in this and began to believe I would prove Mira was more capable than the doctors believed her to be. When I was able to look past all the wires and tubes, I could see my baby girl.

I would eventually discover that what I was really struggling with was the fear that, beyond Mira's condition, I too was broken.

CHAPTER TWO:

STABILITY ON THE WALL

D read stalked me each time I thought about bumping into the mom at Noah's preschool whose son had been born not long after Mira. I pictured her arriving at the school with her baby in a carrier or stroller, and me empty-handed. While I felt a deep yearning to peek at her new son and congratulate her, I had no idea what to do with my feelings of emptiness and uncertainty. She was aware of the complications at Mira's birth, and I worried about the sadness she might feel for me.

Life had already shown me that we draw into our lives those people and situations that have the potential to reveal aspects of ourselves that may have been buried for years. And then, one morning, this mother was in the classroom with her new baby in a carrier.

Every day the week before, I had felt my gut tighten in anticipation of this moment. I clutched Noah's hand as we walked down the hall to his classroom, hoping once again our arrival would not coincide with hers. On this particular morning, Noah let go and happily ran into his class. I cautiously peeked my head in and scanned the room, stopping short at the sight of the mother lightly bouncing and swaying her body with her brand-new baby boy. We locked eyes and froze in place, neither of us knowing who should walk toward whom. Heat rose in my chest and my palms broke into a sweat. She looked just as startled as I did. I wondered if she had also secretly dreaded the day when we would meet.

Gently placing her baby into his stroller, she extended one arm to me as she pushed the stroller with the other and moved toward me. I could see the compassion in her eyes and opened my arms, welcoming her hug. Sadness, grief, congratulations, guilt, worry and compassion swirled around us together. We hugged in silence, neither of us knowing what to say. Then we cried together, each of us feeling seen and understood. Our gentle but heartfelt embrace communicated everything we both needed to move through the moment.

My chest softened and an internal release moved through my ribcage. The part of me that wanted to zip up my feelings, to be able to congratulate her and tell her I was OK, shifted aside to receive the kindness of her gesture, saying without words, *I see you. I am here for you. This must be so hard.*

The collapse I feared didn't happen. Instead, I was able to let just enough of my pain release from the tap without cascading into a waterfall. It wasn't often that I allowed myself to feel painful feelings in the company of others. For most of my life, I held myself together to be the person I thought my parents needed me to be. In my family, there had been little room for my pain and big feelings, so I locked them away. But I kept the key. In this moment, I felt the little girl I'd stuffed away begin to emerge. The experience of shedding tears without falling apart was strangely freeing, cleansing and empowering. I was receiving the comfort that I longed for as a child.

I was coming to realize I had followed in my mother's footsteps and her mother's before, learning to place more importance on the wishes and expectations of others than on expressing my authentic voice.

* * *

Speaking up to authority was something I began stifling many years ago. When I was 7 years old, my father offered to buy me something special if I would swim the length of the swimming pool without grabbing on to the side. "You can do it," he urged. "If you do it today ..." He offered a prize I don't recall.

I wanted to please my dad, and I didn't want my sister to call me a chicken, so I jumped in, submerging my body to adjust to the cold water. I began to swim, suppressing with each stroke of my arm my increasing desire to grab hold of the side of the pool. My arm shook with the impulse to reach for the security of the wall, but my father was watching. My chest was tight, which made my breath shallow, but I knew he would be disappointed if I didn't make it to the end of the pool.

Though my father was self-assured in many ways, he had never learned to swim. My mother couldn't swim either. Now, they were asking me to accomplish what neither of them could do. It's common for parents to unconsciously attempt to fulfill their desires and dreams through their offspring, but it places an unwarranted burden on the children.

Though I can't recall the reward, I clearly remember the tension of forcing my body to disobey its own impulses. I had no wish to become a successful swimmer and no particular love of swimming. I chose to ignore my feelings so that I could fulfill my parents' wishes. To this day I'm not a confident swimmer and I am not at ease in large bodies of water where there is no edge to grasp. The discomfort both my parents felt around water settled more deeply into my body than the confidence they tried to instill in me.

Instead of feeling empowered, I felt resentful of my parents' need to have children who could swim. As an adult, mother, therapist and conscious parenting coach, I have come to recognize the many incidents in my childhood and those of my clients that have taught us—women especially—to silence our voices and stuff down our feelings in the presence of perceived authority.

We all need different levels of support when it comes to letting go of control and trusting our body to navigate the waters, whether they be ocean waves or ripples in a lake or swimming pool. How would swimming feel now had I been allowed to use the side of the pool as long as I needed? I believe if I was encouraged to swim independently and grow naturally, alongside feelings of trust and belief from my father, I could have let go of the side on my own timeline. While my father's intention was pure and well-meaning, it also robbed me of the experience of learning to trust myself.

On that day in the NICU, when the neurologist failed to offer consolation or make a meaningful connection as he delivered the news about Mira, a quiet voice began to bubble up from deep within my belly. That voice was beginning to claim its right to exist. And while I hadn't found that strength earlier, now I felt empowered.

Days later, I spoke with the head neonatologist for the NICU, who exuded warmth and caring, as well as respect. As my eyes filled with tears, he wrapped his arm around my shoulder, and we walked down a long hallway to his office. "I will not let you leave this NICU before I have you set up with a neurologist that I would send my own children to for care," he promised.

* * *

A fighting spirit began to rise in me like none I had ever felt. I was determined that Mira and I would challenge attitudes about brain trauma in newborns. I was convinced that my connection to and belief in her was stronger than any doctor's evaluation. I was ready to do everything possible—research, advocacy, every therapy under the sun—to give Mira the best life she could have. We would defy anyone's predictions about what Mira would do and accomplish. I was going to do parenting a child with cerebral palsy right, and I would not disappoint.

What I didn't understand at the time was that I was pulling Mira into my expectations, hopes and dreams, blinded by a deep-seated belief that the goal was to get her as close to "typical" as possible. The specter of losing that fantasy was terrifying to me. There was a lurking sense of grief and pain that I feared, if released, was not survivable. So instead I shifted seamlessly into the role of fixer and got busy fending off the enemy.

Mira continued to gain stamina and wean herself off each tube in the NICU. Day after day, her body resting on mine, our abdomens pressed together, my breath finding the rhythm of her breath, hers finding the rhythm of mine, we grew to know each other. The milk from the bottle and my breast was teaching her she did not need to rely on the external support of machines. The presence of our true human connection called forth her internal strength.

Three weeks into her residence, she was only connected to the monitors and one last small clear tube through her nose that provided the nourishment she needed until she got enough of her milk from my breast and the bottle. I was finally able to hold her freely, without fear of disconnecting any wires. Every few days, the staff moved her crib closer to the entrance. With each move, we were another step closer to leaving the NICU.

Many years earlier, as I was learning to do a headstand in yoga, sirsasana, I was afraid to fall. I first practiced the inversion with my legs against the wall, and with each new attempt I moved a little further away and into a freestanding pose. Through practice, I learned to feel through my fear of falling and call upon my inner strength and stability, which held my excitement and sense of confidence.

Leaving the NICU was like moving away from that wall all over again. The danger of any external prop is that we can become too dependent on it. I had grown reliant on the NICU staff and the monitors to show me what I needed to do. Like doing a headstand without the wall, I needed to learn that I could find balance on my own.

As the day of our departure approached, my excitement was contaminated with concern. As much as I was ready to go, anxiety stirred within me concerning my ability to care for Mira on my own, even with the support and help of my husband. Part of me was content with her staying in the hospital. I'd grown used to the routines, so it seemed normal for me to be there.

What made the doctors and nurses think I was capable of caring for Mira without the support of the NICU? How could they send Mira home without a nurse? Perhaps we could take a monitor with us for a while? I had become so accustomed to tracking her vitals on machines, I was anxious about how I'd know what to do if something was off. I worried we didn't have enough support at home. We'd only just left our community in Madison, Wisconsin, and the sum of my newly formed community was right here at Beth Israel Hospital in Brookline, Massachusetts.

"She's not a NICU baby anymore," nurse Nancy said to me one day. I knew she was right. But even if Mira was no longer a NICU baby, I had become a NICU mom. I needed to find the belief within myself that I could care for this child on my own.

At home, there had been daily knocking on our door from parents of children in Noah's preschool class, delivering meals, desserts and basic supplies. As I received each delivery, I was growing comfortable with my emerging community and accepting their help.

* * *

As we settled into our new routine outside of the hospital, I longed to reconnect with yoga and occasionally found moments to engage in my practice. I had done so off and on since graduate school while I earned a master's degree in psychology and drama therapy. For me, it was mostly a physical practice at the time, and I had always enjoyed warrior II pose. The pose requires both feet to be fully planted, feeling all three points of each foot rooting into the ground. Leaning into a bent front leg, you also send your energy and attention to the back leg, which is straight. When done correctly, this pose brings forth a moment-to-moment awareness of all aspects of your stance, alignment and breath. It calls on inner and physical strength, balance and stability. Despite its name, this pose is not about struggle. In order for it to be a complete asana, or yoga pose, one must find the surrender within warrior II.

From childhood into adulthood, I had often taken on a rigid warrior stance, one that held no joy or ease, zipping up any sense of vulnerability, holding my breath and powering through. Learning to parent Mira in the days, weeks and months after leaving the NICU would challenge me to develop strength born of flexibility and ease of stance. As in warrior II pose, I would need to practice reaching for what was behind me while moving toward what was ahead.

There were times throughout this journey when a voice deeper than words spoke up, assuring me that Mira was a complete person beyond what her body and mind might be capable of. I didn't yet have the language to describe this understanding, but it was a feeling in the depths of my heart—a sense of knowing, with a heartbeat all its own.

Because it was an internal truth and not objective, I was easily swept back into a state of comparison and worry whenever I was out in the world with Mira. That's when stories about what others were thinking crept in. My thoughts spiraled into scenarios of disappointment, even catastrophe. *What if she never walks? What if she never sits up by herself? What if she's never able to speak? She'll have no friends, no ability to interact with her brother or cousins,* I thought.

I would continue to return to warrior II, and draw from that internal strength, as I learned to mother Mira.

CHAPTER THREE:
IN SEARCH OF BALANCE

A few months after we brought Mira home, we enrolled her in a state-run early intervention program that provided developmental assessments for children, as well as physical therapy, occupational therapy and speech therapy—all of which I knew little about.

This meant that throughout Mira's infancy and early childhood, there were regular visits from different therapists who came to our home to work with her. They became my teachers and guides—the experts who modeled what I needed to do with her. Observing the physical therapist place her hands on Mira's leg, lift it and rotate or stretch it, I learned how to do the same. From the occupational therapist, I learned how to hold Mira while feeding her. Each therapist carried knowledge I was desperate to acquire. I tried to memorize each stretch or exercise.

Despite not having any formal training, my inner perfectionist insisted that I do it all and do it right. I devised my own prescription for Mira's success, saddling myself with an ever-growing to-do list, attempting to incorporate everything I was learning into my daily care for my daughter. I longed to be told what to buy and what needed to be done to ensure everything turned out right. I feared that each day handled less than perfectly would translate into a missed opportunity for Mira to learn another skill.

At the end of many of the sessions, I'd stand at the door of our home as various therapists packed up the toys, books and training materials they'd brought with them. "Is this an item we should own?" I would ask, grasping for guidance regarding what to buy as if seeking a magic pebble that would enable Mira to succeed. I began to wonder if the therapists were instructed not to advise clients on which items to purchase, because each one managed to escape our conversations without ever saying, "Yes, it's a must!" or even, "Yes, it would be a good idea."

My relentless search for knowledge was fueled by anxiety. If there was a right therapy or therapeutic toy, then there also had to be a wrong one. This right-wrong thinking was a continual source of stress. And I lived with a chronic sense of responsibility, which mandated that we never miss a session of physical, speech or occupational therapy.

I also continued to look for the silver lining. During the therapists' visits, I would observe how calm they were with

Mira. Knowing these trusted allies were as invested in achieving positive outcomes for Mira as I was helped calm me as well. Observing the therapists filled me with optimism. I believed the therapies would make Mira the strongest child she could be. I thought it would help her avoid surgeries and meet her developmental goals.

I lived for the moments when I was alone with Mira or walking with her strapped to my chest; the feeling of her body next to mine reassured me. And when she eventually gave us a smile and followed us with her eyes, I was elated. Her expression gave me a window into her soul, and I deeply appreciated the ease of this connection. It gave me hope she could continue to progress, even if on her own timeline.

I didn't understand yet that this was idealizing the typical, suspending my fear of our future, convincing myself that all was going to be fine.

* * *

"How old is she?" a mother seated across from me asked as she handed her toddler one plastic toy at a time. She was keeping him occupied as they waited for the pediatrician's nurse to call them in for their appointment.

"She's 8 months," I responded and waited silently for the next question: Is she your first? Is she sitting yet? Does she sleep through the night? Where did she get all that hair?

For most parents, these are routine questions they take pleasure in answering. For me, they were a source of angst. Some days I explained why Mira wasn't sitting yet. Other days the questions gutted me, and I could barely speak. Today was one of those days.

The mother flashed an uncomfortable smile and switched her focus back to her little boy, who was in need of a new object for the dollhouse. I was grateful she had a reason to divert her attention. Exercising control over what and how much I told people was comforting—I certainly didn't have control over much else in Mira's life.

Sitting in the doctor's office always brought me to that humbling place where "something is wrong with us" flashed like a neon sign inside my brain. One of the main reasons we bring our babies to the doctor during these first few years is to check off the achievements or developmental milestones. For Mira, we seldom checked any of those boxes.

Each time we visited the doctor, Mira underwent a battery of tests. We wondered if she would pass or fail, or if she was growing. During this visit, the growth tests were fine, except for her head circumference. Then the doctor tested her head lag, holding Mira's hands and pulling her into a sitting position. Her head should have followed up into a vertical position, but it didn't.

With each developmental milestone Mira wasn't reaching, the difference between a typical child and Mira became more clearly marked. Instead of just accepting it, I put more pressure on myself. I thought it was my job to help her catch up. A chronic and exhausting sense of responsibility was mounting.

After another visit to the doctor, as I walked home with Mira, it occurred to me that the physician hadn't adjusted Mira's seizure medication despite her gain in weight. I immediately called the office and spoke with a nurse. She relayed my concern, and the doctor confirmed that Mira's medication dosage needed to be increased. In this uncharted territory with no map to follow, I realized I needed to monitor not only my child but her doctors as well. I realized it was yet another duty in my new role of child advocate and started the search for a new doctor.

* * *

I began bringing Mira to weekly mother and baby groups at a local toy store. The store's owner provided coffee and muffins for moms and babies in the neighborhood—it was a great place to sit together and get to know one another. But it was also a place to compare the babies against each other. There was always discussion about the cute factor of the babies' clothes, hair and eyes, as well as talk of developmental milestones.

Sitting in this circle of moms and babies, I longed to connect with other women. Yet it was hard to feel like Mira and I fit in. When I explained our situation to the moms, the response I received was most often one of sadness. And a pity party wasn't something I was looking for. Baby groups became just one more place that left me feeling a bit broken and on my own.

I played mind games with myself by setting what I believed were more realistic dates for Mira to achieve various milestones. Maybe at 3 she would be able to sit up on her own. Perhaps she would stun everyone by suddenly talking at age 6 or 7. I knew the absurdity of setting these timelines and privately wondered: *What if she never sits up on her own? What if she never reaches any of these milestones? Then what?*

As I left the grocery store one afternoon with Mira strapped in the BabyBjörn, I glanced at the community bulletin board and noticed a yoga class for parents and babies one town over in Watertown. The thought of it intrigued me, but I had no idea if or how I would be able to do yoga with Mira.

Nevertheless, the following Tuesday morning at 10 a.m., Mira and I entered a sunny yoga studio next to an Armenian grocer that sold hummus and muhammara, a delicious dip made from walnuts, pomegranates, spices and oil. Yoga mats were spread out on the clean wood floor of the studio. Relaxing music played through a sound system in the back room.

Laura, the teacher, greeted each mom and baby as they entered the space. Once we were all seated on our mats, she welcomed us and explained that she would demonstrate the yoga poses for our babies using a long-legged and long-armed stuffed frog. Though I was new to such an environment and a bit nervous, I felt strangely at home in this sunlit space of clean wood floors, Krishna Das playing in the background, and the bubbly and warm presence of the instructor.

The class began with us chanting "Om Shanti, Hari Om," and I smiled to myself recalling my first experience chanting several years ago at the Integral Yoga Center in San Francisco while in graduate school. I found the chanting too esoteric at the time and not for me. But this particular morning I was more open and trusting, willing to revisit the chanting with a beginner's mind. Surrounded by other women and their babies, I was among kindred new moms who were trying to learn how to be in the present moment with their babies, doing something healthy for themselves and seeking connection.

Yoga class consisted of a mix of poses for the moms, while our babies lay on their backs with their heads supported by a Boppy pillow. We did planks and downward dogs as our babies watched our faces. After we practiced for a while, we moved on to doing yoga with our babies. Supporting one of their hips with our hands, we lengthened the other leg. We assisted their bent knees into side twists. We helped them into bridge poses. We eventually brought them onto our legs, bending our knees while slowly elevating them into an inversion pose. Some babies fussed, some preferred to be next to their mom, and others returned to their Boppy. At the end of the class we placed our babies on our stomachs, their backs to our bellies, for deep relaxation. I didn't get to know the other moms in the yoga class, but I didn't feel like Mira and I stood out as we had in the mom and baby group at the toy store.

Toward the end of the series, I spoke with Laura about the possibility of continuing to work with Mira. I wanted more and felt on a deep level that yoga was calling us. I loved that it was something we could do together, something that had benefits for both of us that I wouldn't fully understand until later. Yoga felt familiar, as if it was drawing out a source of knowledge I already possessed.

Laura offered to work privately with us. One morning a week, Mira and I visited Laura at her home, where she welcomed us with beautiful yoga music and delicious chai. Laura moved Mira through various stretches and poses. The two of them grew close as I looked on, sipping my tea. Afterward, Mira and I would do deep relaxation together. I'd lay on my back with Mira also on her back, lying on my belly. After a few moments, Mira's breathing tuned in to the rhythm of mine. I would rejoice at her deep breaths, feeling the way her entire body had become relaxed.

In these moments, as I tuned in to my breath, all of my fears of the future vanished, eclipsed by an uncomplicated and powerful presence with Mira—our soul-to-soul connection.

* * *

We stood in a parking lot in a wooded area over an hour away from home, about to go for a walk with Noah, his preschool friend and her father. When I opened the rear door of the car where Mira was strapped safely into her seat, I quickly noticed her eyes were twitching and her lips were rhythmically smacking.

I looked at Marc, who was standing 10 feet away from the car. "Mira's having a seizure," I told him. The words left my lips softly, but I was feeling anything but calm. Our gazes locked for a moment, as if we each hoped the other could make this stop.

Mira was 9 months old and had been seizure-free since she left the NICU. I had no clue how far we were from a hospital. Time began to move in freeze-frames. My knees began to tremble, and I felt lightheaded and weak. Noah and his friend looked on, their eyes wide.

Marc swooped in like a divine intervention, removing Mira from her car seat and holding her on her side just like we had been told to do. My shaky hand held the phone as I spoke to our new doctor with a trembling voice. Before leaving Noah's preschool classroom one morning, I had approached a father who I knew was a pediatrician and kindly—and maybe somewhat desperately—asked if he would be willing to take Mira as one of his patients. With compassionate eyes and half a smile, he replied, "I am disposed to take her."

I had felt some relief, but I was not sure what he meant and was too embarrassed to ask. I had walked as quickly as I could back home and asked Marc what he thought the doctor meant by "disposed." He had assured me we'd found a new doctor.

Now, settling my feet firmly on the ground beneath me, I took in the directives from him. "I want you to take her to the nearest hospital. She is likely to have more seizures, so she should be watched. I think we will need to get her back to Boston by ambulance so I can see her tomorrow."

I absorbed his words as if he was talking to someone else and referring to someone else's story. This was not my story. I didn't know the little girl we were talking about. I didn't know myself as a mother of a child who had seizures.

In truth, Mira and seizures were no strangers. She had multiple seizures during the first days of her life. She had been given medication to prevent further seizure activity, but over time the medication began to destroy her teeth. When we realized what was happening, we switched medications, but the new one decreased her appetite, making it challenging to get her all the medicine she needed. I felt anxious feeding her, knowing she had to finish the entire bottle of milk because it contained the medicine. Instead of being present in the moment, enjoying the process of feeding her, I was tense. I yearned for the joyful image of feeding my baby I had experienced before her medication and that I had with Noah. I started to dread her feedings because I was filled with what-ifs and a whole bottle's worth of anxiety.

After changes in Mira's behavior, longer periods of sleep, lethargy and loss of exuberance, we took her off the second medication as well. I foolishly began to assume that seizures were a thing of the past.

Now I wondered if this seizure would just stop on its own. Would she continue to seize at the hospital? Would she suffer more brain damage? One moment we were opening the car door, preparing to take a walk in the woods with our children and friends like any ordinary family. The next we were back in the world of white-coated doctors, beeping machines and the land of brokenness. It stung like a slap in the face, a wake-up call that I needed to face reality once more and grapple with my fear of the unknown.

Dom, Noah's friend's father, was a source of calm in the storm. He beckoned his daughter and Noah to his side and managed to keep them entertained with leaves and rocks, while helping Marc and I decide our next move.

At the Cape Cod hospital, we were greeted with a message that Mira's doctor was sending an ambulance to bring Mira to Boston Children's Hospital. Her current seizure had stopped. She looked tired but was back to herself. However, the doctor believed she was likely to have another seizure and wanted to do more tests.

Dom took his daughter and Noah out for pizza, while Marc and I waited for the ambulance to lead us back to Boston. I felt grateful for a friend who was able to think clearly and take care of Noah. It allowed us to focus on Mira.

* * *

While my hands held the two plastic cups suctioned to my breasts, and the loud humming of the breast pump filled the living room, Noah's eyes locked onto mine. "Can you play with me, Mommy?" he asked.

I could barely hear his voice over the sound of the breast pump. "Not right now. I have to pump milk for Mira," I said.

His chin dipped ever so slightly as he set his stuffed animal and book down on the floor and disappeared from view. It had begun to feel like a common refrain. There was a cinching of my gut for having to say no. But just as painful was the helplessness of not being able to offer a comforting touch. In an instant, the pride I'd felt for being able to make milk to nourish my baby plummeted and formed a barrier between my son and myself.

Before this, I hadn't considered that as an only child, Noah mostly received what he wanted and needed when he wanted and needed it. When he was hungry, I fed him. When he cried, I swooped in to stop the crying. During the first six months of his life, when we lived in Brooklyn, New York, I'd walk and ride the subway everywhere with Noah strapped to my chest. Standing in a herd of people in a crowded subway, I'd wiggle my way toward the train so Noah could see his reflection in the window as it pulled up. He'd bounce with excitement in his BabyBjörn as the train sped along the tracks.

Noah and I attended mommy and baby groups in Manhattan where the leader assured new mothers it was OK to let the dishes sit in the sink—they weren't going anywhere. This wasn't exactly comforting to me as I knew I would be the one to have to clean them eventually. Still, I heard the message loud and clear that interacting with my baby was the most important thing I could do, and the dishes could wait. And because I wanted to get this motherhood thing right, I spent almost every waking hour interacting with Noah.

I hesitated to raise my hand when the leader of the group asked how many of us had babies who slept through the night. A colorful mobile hung above Noah's crib. It was not as intricate as the one my new friend from the group made from collected twigs, leaves and beads, but Noah's played music. At 8 p.m. each night, we laid him on his crib mattress and turned on the mobile. His gaze followed the floating objects as they circled, captivating him until he drifted off to sleep. I spent hours reading to him, both of us on our backs, me holding the board book above his face. I narrated the entire day as I folded laundry, cleaned the apartment and gave him a bath. When I was tired of talking, we played music. If I wasn't interacting with him, I was observing him.

Noah was easy. He had a gentle demeanor from day one. As my mom continually praised me for my dedication to constant interaction, and others remarked how happy he was, I patted myself on the back. I believed I must have been doing a hell of a good job.

As he grew, Noah gained a reputation as the kid in the neighborhood whom parents wanted their children to play with. Even spirited kids played nicely with Noah. Siblings got along well when he was in the mix. He was a kind soul who never uttered the word "mine," which would have been totally normal for a 2-year-old claiming ownership of a toy another child was playing with. When a kid took something Noah was playing with, he'd notice and simply pivot to play with something else. He received the title of "Zen Child" by the time he was in preschool because of his demeanor.

I often wondered how much of this was his natural essence, how much was the result of never having anything to get upset about, and how much was a tendency he'd inherited from me to be agreeable in order to avoid hurt feelings. Despite his calm presence, with Mira now in our world, and my inability to provide for him in the ways we'd both become accustomed to, I wondered if he might grow angry toward me and resentful of Mira.

Year after year, I expressed only one concern to Noah's schoolteachers. I feared he wasn't speaking up for himself due to the high needs of his sister. His teachers assured me that Noah spoke up for what he needed. They also described him as someone they could see meditating on a mountaintop.

I began to wonder if it's a parent's responsibility to give the child everything they need. How are we, as parents, able to discern what they need from what we think they need? I witnessed my discomfort and feelings of inadequacy in those moments when I was not available to Noah, and then I unconsciously allowed those judgments to make me feel like I was not enough.

On some level, I knew the pain and fear of letting one child down when another child entered the family was typical. I also knew simply strapping a second child to my chest, pushing the other in the stroller, and repeating old patterns, but now with two, was not realistic. It certainly wouldn't be sustainable with Noah and Mira. The mere thought of taking them both to the playground heightened my anxiety. What if Mira struggled to drink the milk with her seizure medication and we needed to return home to ensure she got it? What if Mira had a seizure and Noah didn't want to leave? My mind was constantly flooded with images and scenarios in which my time with Noah might be interrupted because of Mira.

CHAPTER FOUR:
GIVE ME YOUR HAND

The parent and baby yoga classes with Laura introduced me to a world of healing modalities that weren't based on the idea that my daughter was broken and needed to be fixed. They inspired me to explore a variety of approaches, including body-mind centering work, craniosacral therapy, Watsu massage therapy, music therapy and eventually horseback riding to help Mira strengthen her core muscles. I learned to follow Mira's lead, sticking to the things she responded to instead of relying on medications and goals to make things different.

I became keenly aware of how these alternative modalities affected Mira as well as myself. I could see it not only in the way the therapist engaged with her, but also in the way Mira responded. And subsequently, in how I felt within myself and about her after each session. These sessions were less goal-oriented and started wherever Mira was at in the moment, allowing movement to happen organically rather than someone moving her body for her.

Mira was always excited when I brought her in for craniosacral therapy, a gentle hands-on treatment focused on places in and around the central nervous system where fluid is blocked. Mira bounced in my arms as I walked up the stairs to the session. As I carried her out afterward, her body was as relaxed as a wet noodle. It was only after these sessions that Mira ever fell asleep in the car. Of all the therapies we tried, it was the hardest to understand intellectually and the most challenging to explain to others. But the witnessing of Mira's enjoyment and relaxation during and after craniosacral therapy was something that remained special between the two of us.

At the start of Watsu therapy, Mira's body was as stiff as a board. In 95-degree water, the therapist gently guided her shoulder in one direction, and Mira's entire body moved rigidly with that shoulder. As the session progressed, Mira relaxed so that when the therapist led or moved her shoulders in one direction, her hips moved from side to side in relaxed opposition. Every now and then, I'd hear her take a deep inhale and exhale.

One day Laura and I were visiting in her kitchen after a yoga session. We were drinking tea and I was talking about my sense of overwhelm at managing all of Mira's therapies and medications, while also trying to be a good parent to Noah.

"You need more yoga in your life," Laura commented. She told me about her own teacher, Sonia Sumar, founder of Yoga for the Special Child.

Since the start of the parent-baby class, Laura had given me illustrated worksheets from her training with Sonia so I could do poses at home with Mira. I decided it was time for me to learn more about the teacher behind this special approach to yoga.

At home, I looked up Yoga for the Special Child and saw that alongside deepening my own yoga practice, I would be able to learn about yoga for children with disabilities. I was relieved to see that the training took place in Evanston, Illinois, and the studio was only five blocks away from my brother's home. *This will be easy,* I thought. *I can walk to class every day.*

I battled the internal voices telling me how selfish it would be to leave my kids and husband for a full week. I saw the complicated logistics that either Marc or our sitter would have to cover, getting Noah back and forth to school and being present for all of Mira's therapies. These voices were loud, but thankfully my intuition was louder. With Marc's full support, I registered for the weeklong introductory training.

* * *

Several months later, I found myself in a training group composed of professionals from the world of special needs and a few parents like myself. I walked to the studio each morning.

As I entered the building and made my way up the carpeted stairs, the smell of incense was a stark contrast to the chilly air outside. I felt the shift from the sounds of the city and external stimulation to my inner experience, feeling my feet meet each step, my arm pulling out from each jacket sleeve. I was aware of the calm and quiet of the studio even as others entered the building.

Leaving the studio for lunch after the morning session on our first day, I walked outside and into a gust of wind that was so bitter it took my breath away. Many of us returned to class holding cups of tea, hoping to warm ourselves, and regrouped in a large circle. The room's white walls and purple carpet exuded an atmosphere of calm, peace and playfulness.

Sonia announced that her car had been towed at some point during the morning. "I went to feed the meter only to find that my car wasn't there," she said with a wide smile. "I love the image of my car getting a tour of the city in upward dog!"

I was stunned by her light hearted reaction, but I was also intrigued by her sense of calm. "It's about accepting the 'as-is' of life," she explained.

As a teacher, Sonia connected deeply with each student as if seeing into our essence and understanding how each movement of our body was an expression of our strengths and our challenges. At the end of each class, lying in savasana, a final resting pose, I found myself in quiet tears. I wasn't sad or overwhelmed but simply beginning to tune in to my authentic self. My body, completely relaxed, allowed the emotions to flow. Distancing myself from the ever-tantalizing distractions, to-do lists and judgments, I was keeping company with my core sense of self.

Throughout the week, I observed self-judgment rising to the surface as a neighbor floated easily into a headstand or lingered effortlessly in a forward bend. I worked on sitting up tall in dandasana without the support of my hands behind me, and I slowly released my upper body forward into paschimottanasana, a seated forward bend, without hunching over. The most difficult poses for me were always the ones that challenged me to surrender and let go.

Sonia reiterated many times throughout the training, "Every child, despite any physical limitations, cognitive limitations or emotional challenges, is a perfectly intact soul."

Sitting in this space and hearing these words created a profound shift in my thinking. It made perfect sense to me and helped me clarify the confusion I often felt with Mira. *Yes! Like every single human and animal, she is a perfectly intact soul!* We are all housed within our unique bodies, and many bodies come with challenges. I realized that deep inside Mira is whole, and that part of her is not only untouchable, but it is the part of her that is radiant and connected to me in the deepest way.

Outside of the group training, these thoughts easily evaporated. As I walked back to my brother's apartment after class one day, I noticed a family of four. Observing the warm connection between the siblings, a voice in my head told a story about all the things my family would never enjoy. The voice prodded me with questions: *Will Noah and Mira have such a connection? Will they ever be able to have a conversation together? Will my family be able to walk down the street like this family, with everyone participating in a conversation?*

This moment was deeply unsettling. It was also the beginning of a transformation within me. It was the first time I told myself with real understanding: *Yeah, you don't know. You don't know what it's going to be like, so you better get used to being in the moment.*

* * *

After my week in Chicago completing the basic certification for Yoga for the Special Child, I was excited to practice what I had learned on Mira. Sonia emphasized the importance of working on Mira's feet. I would start by taking her ankle in one of my hands and holding the top half of her foot with my other hand until I felt her muscles relax. Then I would gently rotate the top half of her foot in circles. I also rubbed my thumbs along the sole of her foot, giving stimulus input. I would place my fingers in between her toes, gently stretching them and creating more space between them. Sonia had taught us that the feet are connected to every organ in the body and how by stimulating the soles of her feet I could stimulate Mira's organs and work on her spine.

At the next session with Barbara, Mira's physical therapist, I talked a mile a minute—something I do when I'm excited. I showed her the technique I'd learned to massage Mira's feet, the proper direction of upper foot rotation, circling each toe, and talking with Mira about each movement so that she could understand and participate. Sonia would tell the children she worked with that she would do 50 percent of the work and they must do the rest.

I rambled on to Barbara about the concept of soul-to-soul connection and the importance of working from the inside out versus from the outside in. She sat quietly and listened as I tried to explain that, though we were moving parts of Mira's body, the intention was coming first from a place of connection. I explained how I'd imagine the movement coming from within Mira, though it was being assisted from the outside.

Without visibly backing away, I could sense Barbara slowly recoil her attention. I was losing my audience. Was she thinking we were using up time when she could be working on Mira? Did she feel the pressure to get started? Did she not agree with what I was talking about? For a moment I doubted myself. Was what I had just learned truly different from what Mira was already doing?

I knew in my heart that it was. Many physical and occupational therapists who attended the program were moved and transformed by Sonia's work. I realized there was a part of me that wanted reassurance that this idea of soul-to-soul connection was legitimate. I wanted Barbara to be half as excited as I was.

"That's pretty much what I do," she said.

I didn't want to offend Barbara—I adored her. I liked her company, and I appreciated the work she was doing with Mira. But I suddenly realized it might have been too soon to share my enthusiasm for what I had just taken in. I could not adequately express in words what I had experienced—at least not yet.

* * *

Understanding what it means to connect with another soul goes beyond what the eyes can see, the ears can hear and the brain can think. It goes right past all of the crap that accompanies judgment, goes against our preconceived ideas of what people should look like, and makes a straight dive for the essence of a human being. It's a connection with the unique essence that only belongs to that person. When given the space to be seen, heard and understood, it connects one human being to another and creates the conditions for each person to rise.

Even though I started experiencing a deep and powerful connection with Mira in the NICU and in our home, I had been relating to her from the outside in, operating in the mindset of what needed to be done to fix her. As Sonia articulated the quality of a soul-to-soul relationship, it shed a bright light on the truth that Mira was whole exactly as she was. Yes, we needed to give her opportunities to rise and see where she had the ability to grow, but it couldn't come from my husband or me creating the goals or deciding who she was going to be. With my new tools, I would practice the listening touch that Sonia taught, a way of using my senses to guide me in connecting with Mira's internal world. Moving her ankle, arm or leg would no longer be a one-way movement. I would listen, wait and feel for Mira's participation. I would tune in and feel when she made an ounce of movement, and then I would support it.

Most importantly, I intended to connect with her soul first—through speaking, holding, loving and looking into her eyes. Only then would I guide her with movement and breath. It would feel as if we were making the movements together, rather than me doing it to her and for her.

* * *

Eight months later, I was back in Chicago at the yoga studio for a second immersion workshop with Sonia. This time Marc flew in with the kids so Mira could be part of a demonstration. Sonia would work on her for half an hour while our group observed. I felt myself flush with excitement as Sonia sat at Mira's feet and looked into her eyes, a small pillow supporting her head. Mira relaxed as Sonia massaged her feet, explaining to her and to us what she was doing.

"Give me your hand," Sonia directed in her Brazilian accent. Mira reached her right hand up to hold Sonia's thumb. "Now give me your left hand," Sonia said. My heart sank at this request. Mira didn't use her left hand, and I was sure she wasn't going to.

"Mira, give me your left hand," Sonia said again. "I'll do 50 percent and you do 50 percent," she said as she wiggled her fingers above Mira. "I need your left hand."

Now she sang in a lilting, inviting manner, "Mira, give me your left hand. Come, come, bring me your left hand." Mira's eyes were fixed on Sonia, while her ears and body tuned in to both Sonia and the soft sound of Krishna Das playing in the background. Sonia kept wiggling her fingers over Mira, singing the same gentle request.

I stared at Mira's left hand thinking, *Come on Mira, come on,* but also telling myself, *She is not going to do it. She is not going to do it.* My heart sank again.

Then, to my complete amazement, Mira began to move her left hand. As Mira slowly raised her hand, Sonia leaned in closer and extended her own hand to meet Mira's halfway, as promised. Sonia's song evoked a trust in Mira, giving her a belief that she could do this. With their fingers entwined, with Sonia's assistance, Mira stretched her left arm into a full extension.

"It's not that she can't use her left hand," Sonia explained, shifting her gaze from Mira to me. "She just has to learn how."

My entire understanding of yoga was transformed in this moment. I realized that Mira's left hand only needed to be given its own voice. It didn't matter if Mira got the movement right. What mattered was that Sonia's willingness to meet Mira where she was had created a sense of trust and room for new possibilities. Yoga was not about doing or not doing, but rather about embodying a way of acceptance of where one is. We can live in a place of fullness and thanks rather than depletion and scarcity. Gratitude began to overtake my shadows and the sense of brokenness deep within me.

My worried voice went quiet for a time. The way I felt in that yoga studio with Mira in that moment began to feel like a privilege. It was as if she was my doorway into a world full of possibilities, a world I knew very little about. It was because of Mira that I was immersing myself in yoga and in this purple-carpeted room with a woman who was changing my understanding, not just of parenting but of being in the world. I felt myself emerging from a fear that Mira would be a burden.

Witnessing the beautiful connection that formed between Sonia and Mira, I was able to connect with an inner clarity I had been frightened to trust. This would not be the last time I would feel doubt and worry. My fears about who Mira might be, the loss of the family I'd imagined, and the fantasies about how parenting two children should be didn't disappear. But I was gradually beginning to accept that the often-overlooked possibility of deep connection between human beings brought with it incredible possibilities for growth and transformation.

* * *

Mira sat contentedly in her car seat while Noah, strapped into his booster seat, wailed with outstretched arms, expressing his frustration and fear that I was leaving. In a little while, I would be on a plane to Brazil to immerse myself in the next level of Yoga for the Special Child with Sonia. But in this moment of departure, my heart was in my belly. I felt nauseous, ambivalent and fearful.

Several days earlier, I'd sat at the counter of a nearby Cambridge café drawing pictures to match the activity for each of Noah's days that I would be gone. I set up a jar filled with Hershey's kisses, one for each night that I would not be able to kiss him while away. I filled an envelope with knock-knock jokes and riddles for Marc to read to him. I made lists and prepared meals so that Marc wouldn't have extra work. Still, I felt overwhelmed by the idea of letting go of so much.

Marc continued to assure me that he would be OK. He'd seen the shift that took place in me after my first yoga retreat. He noticed I was less reactive, calmer and more accepting. I'd been home a couple days when he encouraged me to go on a yoga retreat whenever I wanted. Sonia's training exposed me to a level of self-care that was vastly different and deeper than anything I had practiced before.

Ten thousand feet above the ground, I finally shed the worry, the control and the disbelief I'd been feeling. My fear became lighter as feelings of excitement and calm took over. I felt a sense of purpose.

In the jungle, Sonia woke us each morning with the chimes of a triangle at 6 a.m. Meditation and yoga started at half past the hour. Waking at 6 or earlier, I had time to sip a delicious cup of coffee and appreciate the tranquil view just beyond my window. The beans were grown and roasted on the property. Enjoying my coffee in this exquisite silence, I felt comforted and cared for knowing that someone had woken even earlier than me to prepare this morning experience.

After coffee, my roommates and I dressed silently, seamlessly sharing a bathroom to brush our teeth and shower. We walked upstairs to the hexagon-shaped, light-filled yoga room and took our place in the circle, beginning breath work and eye exercises led by Sonia. This was followed by meditation and yoga.

I was struck by how supported and connected I felt among a dozen relative strangers who were sitting, chanting and practicing yoga together. No words were needed. Aside from the sound of chanting and yoga instruction, our first few hours of the day were spent in silence. I can't remember a time when I spent three hours without talking in the company of others. This daily routine made space for the yoga philosophy to settle in, and it slowed me down.

I began to feel an inner stillness that allowed me to tune in to myself, to experience myself at a level that went deeper than my identities as a mother, friend, wife, sister or yoga student. Deeper than my degrees, certificates, awards and affirmations. Tuning into myself brought me to my unique individuality, the essence that makes me who I am. It went beyond my hairstyle, my clothing, my home decor. It went directly to who I am beneath any label, identification or thought.

One morning, as I sat outside eating my breakfast in silence and enjoying the simple taste of my food, I felt tears rolling down my cheeks. Rather than tears of sadness, they were tears of relief and appreciation—even joy at my newfound ability to maintain an openhearted awareness of the outside world and how it felt internally. For most of my life, I had blocked out much of the stimulus from the outside world before it could ever reach my heart.

As I watched the sunrise, I heard every sound as the sun rose over the hills. I heard the conversation of the birds, the sounds the retreat workers made as they arrived for work. I enjoyed the brief visits to my chair by the dogs from the center and those that arrived with the workers. I basked in the increasing warmth of the sun as it climbed in the sky. My mind was calm and alert. Slowing down enough to actually take in all of my surroundings made me feel more alive than ever.

Absorbing the power of stillness allowed me to feel the as-is of the world around me, the as-is of myself untethered by thoughts, judgments and the eternal to-do lists. Slowly, delicately, I was unraveling the tight web of needing to fix myself and others. In place of fixing, I was discovering the self-care that's possible when one truly accepts the as-is of each moment and each person.

Later, during a second trip to Brazil, which was required for me to complete my training, we each received our certification as yoga practitioners. As Sonia handed out the certificates, she spoke in her lighthearted way about the seriousness of yoga practice. Several of us were in tears.

"Why are you crying?" she asked. "You need to practice detachment. You have received everything you were meant to receive during this time. Nothing is being taken away. All of the teachings are now in you, and I am still with you even if my physical body is in Florida. Even if this training is over, I'm not far away from you." Sonia embraced each of us with one of her big Brazilian hugs, and I felt our soul-to-soul connection.

I learned that Sonia embodies yoga in a way that's different from someone merely teaching the poses and positions. I discovered that yoga is a way of living in the world with ongoing growth, evolution and the acceptance of the as-is of life. My definition of yoga expanded yet again when Sonia declared that even without a yoga practice, Marc is indeed a yogi because he supports my evolution with yoga.

From Sonia I have learned to trust the stillness. When I am willing to hold a pose, even through discomfort, or sit for moments in silence, it's in these spaces of stillness where I am finally able to feel emotions that need to be felt. Here, I give voice to my true needs. This is where my learning and growth began to accelerate.

CHAPTER FIVE:
STABILITY OFF THE WALL

One afternoon when I was in fifth grade, I came home to my mother's announcement that Dad would not be home for dinner. Her tone implied he'd no longer be coming home for dinner. She didn't say much more, leaving me to wonder whether it was my dad who said he wasn't coming home or Mom who told him he was no longer welcome. I had a lot of questions, but I also knew, without being able to articulate it, that my siblings and I would not discuss what was going on. By the age of 9, I had already absorbed the family taboo against expressing feelings of anger or dissatisfaction.

The next afternoon, in the middle of playing four square during recess, I had to choke back a sudden surge of tears. After taking my turn at the game, I stepped out of line and asked my close friend Jill to walk with me.

"What's wrong?" Jill asked after we'd moved far enough away not to be overheard.

"Nothing," I said at first, wanting that to be enough. After a few moments, I added, "My parents might be getting a divorce."

As we sat on the cement curb that encircled the playground, my emotional state veered between feeling the warmth and support from my friend and a sense of shame and terror that my classmates would see me crying. Or worse, that they might find out what was going on. I believed I would lose all my friends. The shame that spread throughout my body was almost worse than the sadness itself.

It took my parents another six years to actually go through with the divorce. I was 17 by that time and at camp having one of the best summers of my life. After all those years, they drove to the camp and announced that they were ready to go through with it.

Throughout the years they were in limbo, I witnessed my mother's unhappiness at home. I'd long been aware of her struggle to feel good about herself. I knew from one or two stories she shared that her own mother had been critical of her weight and put her on diet pills while she was in high school. It seemed Mom was always dieting and often sought validation from me or my sister.

"Look at me," she'd say, pulling the waistband out from her jeans. "See how much weight I'm losing? I couldn't fit into these a few weeks ago!"

I knew she wanted me to say, "Wow! That's fabulous. I'm so proud of you." But her words, rather than signaling satisfaction with her accomplishment, sounded more like a plea for approval. I wanted her to feel good about herself. I didn't want to be the one to grant her self-worth. It was from my mother, as well as culture, that I learned to be self-critical.

The only place I saw my mother fully express herself was at her shop, Off the Wall, where she sold the work of local artists. In sharp contrast to her demeanor at home, at Off the Wall my mother walked with a graceful certainty as she moved around the store creating displays of art and other items. Setting an object here or there, she would rest her hands on her hips and tilt her head from one side to another, occasionally tapping her toes as she considered the effect of her placement. She would straighten her body in a move that signaled satisfaction, the confidence that it was exactly where that particular piece needed to be. Then she would move on to her next project.

In my last two years of high school, I spent many weekends working alongside my mother at Off the Wall, sometimes at the register, other times boxing and wrapping purchases. During those hours, fragments of happy childhood moments surfaced, memories of playing store when I was 7 or 8, working my toy register or writing up carbon copy receipts.

I enjoyed watching my mother interact with customers, greeting them warmly and always taking an opportunity to learn a little bit about them. She delighted in anyone who needed help finding a gift. She would listen intently and offer ideas, sharing stories of the artist and whatever she knew about the handmade bowl, jewelry, or painted floor mat or card. My mother didn't sell anything she didn't admire, which meant what she told her customers was heartfelt. On many occasions, people with no intention of buying anything entered the store just to visit with my mother and bask in the warmth of her presence.

Sometimes my mother gave me the task of placing certain objects on display, and I would visualize, almost as a video rewind, exactly how she had done this. Holding each piece, I slowed my breathing to the speed of my heartbeat and gazed intently at what I was about to do. Tilting my head to consider, the way my mother did, I felt a sense of ease in my body, a lightness in my hold of the object, a flow from my arms and fingertips as I placed the item in various spaces. I knew when I'd found the right space because something would click inside me. A feeling of relaxation would wash over me, a clear connection between me and the object I was handling. I never doubted myself in these moments.

With little understanding of business, my mother forged lasting relationships with artisans and created a room filled with beauty that drew customers in. It was somewhere she flourished. In this space of her own creation, I was able to observe Mom living in her truth, and she became an inspiration to me. In Off the Wall, she modeled a way for me to connect with myself, looking inward and allowing my artistic abilities and intuitive responses to come to the surface. Later, through Mira's presence in my life, I would learn that this is how we are meant to live the whole of our lives.

I also inherited many of my mother's desires to step outside the box, doing things that most of the kids my age weren't doing—whether it was wearing clothing that was slightly unusual, going to live and study in Israel after graduating early from high school, or taking classes outside the mainstream curriculum at college.

I was drawn to the theater department, yet I didn't take typical acting classes. I took courses such as Javanese Dance Drama and Theater in Education, partly because I was genuinely interested in them and partly because I didn't believe I was good enough to be in the acting groups. Risking failure wasn't my cup of tea.

Theater and drama weren't just topics I studied; they were built into my life from its beginning. Growing up, my mother had various rituals that were evidence of her creative spark, keeping her connected to a core part of herself and igniting the same fire within me.

When I was in my early school years, I often came home to find an unfamiliar object or food item on the kitchen table. The sight of it would stop me in my tracks. My mother was playing a game with us: Who can guess the fruit, vegetable or occasional kitchen gadget? Even if she wasn't in the kitchen or the house, I felt an immediate connection to her, knowing she had placed it on the table with the intention of piquing curiosity in my siblings and me. Later, she would quiz each of us and we would have a food tasting.

I'm certain we were the only family on the block who had a soup tasting spoon in the gadget drawer—a wooden tool with a spoon on each end and a center channel connecting the two. When making soup, we'd dip the larger spoon into the broth and tilt it so the liquid traveled down into the smaller spoon, cooling it just enough to take a taste.

Today, I keep this spoon in my kitchen tool canister. When I pull it out to use it, I am immediately connected to my mother, even though she is no longer with us. In these small moments, she is here with me, despite her lack of physical presence.

* * *

In contrast to her playfulness and curiosity, my mother relied on pills to deaden her emotional pain. Despite many doctors referring her to therapists with whom she would have been able to talk about the source of her unhappiness, she declined the opportunity. Everyone in our family knew she experienced depression, but there was an air of secrecy that made discussion of the topic off-limits. My siblings and I never knew what medications she took, but we knew she was taking them. So many things remained unspoken and unexplained. Yet we absorbed so many messages: Don't talk back. No room for pain here. Being thin is the ideal.

Gradually, my mother spent more and more time in bed. I didn't know it at the time, but she had been going from doctor to doctor for painkiller prescriptions. She would move on as soon as he or she suggested therapy, searching for a new physician willing to prescribe more pills. She may have felt better for a while taking them, but the pain remained inside like a foggy film of dirt, clouding her persona and dimming her light.

Perhaps she didn't realize I was watching as she put various pills in her mouth and sipped her drink. She clearly didn't want to share this information or even to be seen in the act of taking them. At the movies or a restaurant, her hands rooted around her purse as she searched with her fingers for the container of pills, never removing the bottle from her bag. I often felt uneasy and wondered what she was hiding. In her concealment, my mother was modeling shame. She felt that depression and taking medication were to be kept to oneself.

The secrecy surrounding my mother's depression made it harder for us to feel close to her. The self-shaming pushed me away. What I couldn't articulate at the time but already understood was that if she couldn't allow herself to take care of her pain and sadness, she couldn't take care of ours either. I got the message loud and clear that I would have to care for my emotions on my own. Not wanting to be a burden to anyone, I stuffed down all the feelings I could and found that the words "I'm fine" kept others from poking around in them.

My siblings and I distanced ourselves from our mother and each found our own ways to avoid showing or discussing our pain. I grew comfortable in my role as a people pleaser who was always "OK" and "fine." My brother took on the role of the comedian, always finding funny costumes and making us all laugh. My sister discovered she could avoid the stress by spending more time in her room immersed in books. Just as our mother hid her need for medication, we hid our feelings deep within ourselves, hoping they would disappear.

It would take Mira entering my life to reveal how much pain I had pushed down inside myself.

CHAPTER SIX:
KICKING UP SAND

Well into my 20s, I was still working through the emotional fallout of my parents' divorce. My dad was in pain, my mom was in pain, and I, unequipped to accept and handle pain, easily slipped back into my role of caregiver and people pleaser. Each time either of them expressed frustration toward the other, I stuffed my feelings into my pockets, pushing the discomfort away. Believing we had failed as a family, I was filled with resentment, sadness and anger.

Three questions made up my inner soundtrack during those days: *How can I fix them? How will I get through this? Can I handle this?* I carried an invisible weight on my shoulders of my parents' pain and the responsibility to contort my world in ways that would comfort them.

In graduate school, training as a creative arts therapist, I found myself struggling to quiet this inner soundtrack and hear the voice that came from a deeper place within myself. Part of my studies in psychology and drama therapy involved participating in my own therapy once a week. One afternoon, sitting in a session with my therapist, Roz, probably talking circles around myself as I often did, she asked me to lie down on the floor. Surprised but curious, I agreed.

I stretched out on the carpet. Roz sat down behind me and gently placed her hand on my head. We stayed this way for a while, neither of us speaking. The warmth of her hands on my forehead and her compassionate presence enveloped me, softening my tense outer persona and putting all the words and thoughts to rest. While uncomfortable in the stillness, I was a committed rule follower, so I didn't break the silence. In minutes, feelings and tears that hadn't broken their silence for years finally found their way out. Five minutes felt like five hours.

As I left the session that day, Roz gave me an assignment for the week: Spend five minutes a day in silence.

"Can I take a bath?" I asked.

"No," she replied. "I want you to do nothing, to simply sit in silence."

The idea alone felt like torture. I hadn't figured it out yet, but Roz clearly knew that what I needed was to learn to get still. My thoughts and words and actions were like sand kicked up beneath footsteps in the ocean—they'd made everything murky. Only getting still would allow the sand to settle so I could see clearly and get to the bottom.

Years later, after completing Sonia's five levels of training, I started to take on a few clients, teaching Yoga for the Special Child. I usually worked with the child for 30 to 40 minutes and then spent the remaining time talking with and often supporting the mother. I found myself increasingly drawn to working with the parents, but time limits always stifled the conversation from going deeper.

I began leading a group of moms of tweens in a meditation practice that helped them slow down, get quiet and allow what was truly needed in their life to be voiced. We met once a month in a comfortable room with nine plush red BackJack meditation chairs set in a circle on a gray rug. I pulled the shades to provide some privacy from the street and parking lot. I turned the heat up and put calm music on for the mothers who had committed to this first Tuesday of each month.

A woman named Leslie entered first most Tuesdays, said hello with a forced smile and slowly walked over to her seat. She described herself as a glass-half-empty person. Often overwhelmed by her 10-year-old son's behavior, she was frequently reactive and spoke negatively about her kids.

The rest of the moms entered the room, dragging in the baggage of their perpetual exhaustion. Each mom was ready to rant and complain about the behavior of their kids, but that's not what they were here for, and they knew this.

After a few minutes of talking and settling into the circle, I asked everyone to sit in a comfortable position and close their eyes. I asked them to place one hand on their heart, chest or belly and bring their attention to their breath. I instructed, "Note the rise and fall of your chest, the expansion and contraction of your belly."

The sudden halt in chatter opened a space that's rarely available for moms—a chance to step away from the noise and busyness of their lives for a few minutes and tune in to themselves. This time provided an opportunity for their entire being to show up, not just their thoughts and their physical body. I would close my eyes for part of this time, sensing the physical changes happening in the circle. With each exhale, I asked the group to let go of a bit more of their noisy day and all the chatter that followed them into the room. With each inhale, I encouraged them to see if they could simply be in the moment, guiding them, "Bring your attention back to your breath."

Shoulders gently dropped, facial muscles relaxed, and breathing became slower. The length of exhalations increased. There was an energetic shift in the room, from individuals who entered the space with a story or an agenda to pursue to a collective sense of the group—the understanding that we were all moms experiencing the next hour and a half together. The individual parts formed a whole.

As each mom slowly opened her eyes, I saw and felt a readiness to be there, both for receiving and giving. I witnessed a solid strength to their presence and a receptivity to what they were about to experience.

Over the space of several months, I observed a shift in the way they looked at parenting. Instead of complaining about their kids' issues or behavior, they spoke of their own experiences, personal struggles and successes. Their focus turned inward. They could see and support their children and themselves as they explored their own way of being during difficult moments. An environment was created in which the women felt free to open up.

Susan took a breath and said, "I had a really good week. Then, this morning, I lost it with my son because I didn't want him to be late for school." Instead of dwelling on the episode itself, Susan spoke from the heart of that moment, allowing the group to feel the sadness of the experience. The shame she felt around her own agenda began to lift as she told her story. Her eyes became luminous as she connected with her feelings and released herself from the weight of the event.

Susan's story emerged not through ideas, but through emotions that had been in search of a voice. Articulating these pent-up feelings, she was able to feel self-compassion, which allowed others to connect with and support her experience as they began to recognize the pattern in which she'd been stuck. Dropping into these moments of stillness, Susan and each woman in this circle was learning to escape from patterns of reactive behavior, forming new patterns of emotional flexibility and resilience.

In my work as a parenting coach, parents come into my office wanting nothing more than for their children to be happy, confident, resilient and successful. Parents don't realize that through unconscious behaviors—the glances, the tone in their voice, their expectations—they fail to model behavior that will bring their children real comfort. To be truly at home in their own skin, their children must learn what it means to be true to themselves.

I don't question the sincerity of these parents. Their intentions are pure, even when their approaches are misguided. The most difficult task any parent faces is to nurture a child's sense of what's true for them. Children are like sponges, soaking in the energy of the parents' emotional states. When a parent is stressed, anxious, depressed or angry, the child experiences a lack of safety. When we hold emotions that we can't acknowledge, our children not only feel our energy but also absorb those unexpressed tensions in their own body. These eventually settle into the imprint of the child, affecting their sense of themselves.

When we uncover and bring to light the unconscious legacies we have all inherited in one way or another, we can recognize and become aware of all the subtle messages we pass on to our children. We can decide to break deeply ingrained patterns, even as we can choose to build on the ones we want to continue for future generations.

* * *

Marc and I had been kicking around the idea of having a third child. Mira was 4 or 5 at the time, and though we had come to accept she would likely never speak with words, there were times when this truth felt like a gaping wound in the family. It felt especially true for me when I considered her relationship with Noah. They would never be able to have conversations, and I worried about the isolation and loneliness of this divide. I was concerned Noah might feel like he was missing out. A third sibling would be a gift to Noah, not only as a young child but as an adult, as together they could help in caring for Mira. On the other hand, how would I continue to give Mira what she needed if I had another child to parent?

At some level, if not entirely consciously, I understood that part of my attraction to the idea of having another child rested on the notion that I needed to heal the trauma of my last birth. But, if I had finally come to accept Mira as a whole being, as I believed I had, why was I looking to have another child? What was I really looking for?

Conversations and thoughts churned. I recognized the feeling—like stepping into the ocean, kicking up sand. The unwelcome truth was that I wanted to have another "typical" birth experience to assuage some pain within myself. I projected that onto Noah and Marc, creating a story that we all needed the addition of a healthy child to feel complete and to heal from the trauma of Mira's birth. In search of more practical reasons to explain my choice to others, I looked to my family of origin to justify my decision. There are three siblings in my family. We are each three years apart in age. Our birthdays are in three consecutive months. My parents gave birth to my sister three years into their marriage. The number three was familiar to me, and it sounded much better than explaining I wanted to heal my pain by having another child. I would be carrying on a family tradition.

I was also gripped with fears of what-if and tangled myself in the worries of all that could go wrong. What if I followed my belief that Noah would benefit from a neurotypical sibling and then gave birth to a child who had even more health issues than Mira? With all the care Mira required, I sensed my playfulness, my ability to be in the moment, my lightness—the way I felt after returning from my yoga trainings—slipping away. I also felt the rigidity of what I believed we could or could not do as a family, the risks I was willing to take, and the constant weight of always having something to do for Mira that sat upon my shoulders. All of this took me further away from the beautiful and nourishing place of just being.

I needed to stand still in the ocean, to let the sand settle. So I got quiet. Then, on a bike ride with Marc during a weekend getaway, I reconnected with my spirit of lightness and play. Only then did it become crystal clear to me that I wanted to bring another child into our world. Only then could I envision a healthy birth, a playmate for Noah and a future partner in care for Mira. Only then could I imagine chasing and playing with another child and recognize the importance of bringing that playfulness into our family.

I was still fully aware of the possibility that, if this child was also born with health issues, there could be more chaos in our family. Despite all the work with Sonia, I still struggled to accept the as-is of our family's situation and tried to manage every aspect of Mira's life, though it was an impossible challenge to meet. I knew something in me needed to shift. A friend with four daughters had suggested that a third child would force me to shift my attitude, and I finally began to believe it. I needed to learn how to take care of myself first and accept that some of my children's needs would have to remain unmet.

We are taught from a young age that a good mother gives of herself and puts her children first above all else. A selfless mother has been the gold standard. But a selfless mother is exactly that—self-less. The external circumstances needed to be extreme enough to push me to a place where I had no choice but to let go of this idea in order to survive. Up to this point, I hadn't been able to make that decision as a choice. I didn't believe I had permission. I was finally ready.

* * *

"You have a healthy baby boy!" the nurses announced. I felt a rush of relief that shot from my head through my throat and down to the deepest part of my gut, an inner and outer exhale like an enormous wave crashing upon the shore and then gracefully sliding back into the sea.

I had the support of midwives for my first two pregnancies, and I was grateful for them. With my third child, I went all-in with Western medicine and a preventative mindset. I did every possible test, and I carried a load of worry about the pregnancy that I hadn't even known was possible with Noah and Mira. This time, I controlled whatever I could. With the birth of Noah, I didn't use any pain medication. With Mira, I didn't have a choice. With this pregnancy, I experienced delivery with an epidural. With a preplanned date and time, the doctor induced me when he thought I was ready.

When our son was born weighing 8 pounds 14 ounces, the pediatrician said, "Wow! I didn't expect a baby that size to come out of you!" With his glistening red hair and solid build, we initially called him Rufus. During the pregnancy, we had fun coming up with silly names and joked that if he came into the world with red hair, we would name him after Rufus Wainwright. So for the first few days, despite his given name being Micah Benjamin, we called him Rufus.

By 8 months, Micah was pulling himself up on everything. Mastering the art of gibberish, he would stand in his crib, using one hand for balance and the other to emphasize his message, giving full-on sermons with an intonation of passion, strength and righteousness. It was completely unintelligible to any of us but clearly important to him.

Having Micah was, in fact, healing for me, just not in the way I thought it might be. He did bring out the playfulness in me and also challenged me to look at myself, though perhaps in more subtle ways than Mira did. But it was because of Mira that I was able to challenge myself with Micah, rather than be challenged by him. I found I could take pauses; I could see him and his tantrums as his obstacles to work through and not mine to fix. I could listen to his commands and requests, and before shooting them down because I was the parent and he needed to listen to me, I could take his words in, sit with them, and respond to him as a full human, soul to soul. I could do so with his own wholeness pulsing within his little body, while also taking care of myself and the emotions that arose for me. I learned to respond to him in ways he truly needed rather than with reactions dictated by culture and tradition. Because of Mira, I was able to see Micah's intensity simply as part of who he was.

CHAPTER SEVEN:
BATHROOM DOORS

A s sheets of Charmin slid back and forth under the bathroom door with written messages between my mother and me, I felt my anger at her begin to soften into amusement. For the past hour, I'd been bombarding her with pleas and arguments as to why she should let me attend an evening Jewish social event on a school night, which I emphatically believed deserved a yes.

"I promise, I'll be home by 10:30," I said.

"No," she replied.

"This is your fault anyway for sending me to a Jewish camp." Very few of my school friends were Jewish, and then one summer she signed me up for camp and told me I was going less than a week before it began.

"No," she said again.

I was now talking to a locked door and could no longer see her face. Locking herself inside the bathroom sent a clear message she was done and didn't want to listen anymore. But I was not done talking. And because she wasn't going anywhere and I sat outside the door, we remained connected.

I continued to plead my case. "So now I have Jewish friends and want to see them and you're not letting me! You make no sense!"

Realizing that I was not backing down or walking away, she continued the discussion, just not in a way that I expected—a piece of toilet paper pushed underneath the door with writing on it. I was so taken aback by this twist in the scene that the lines I had been playing over and over again, like a broken record, stopped suddenly. My mother threw an improvisational curveball, and I needed to shift my thinking in order to respond.

I imagined her smile on the other side of the door as she came up with this clever tactic. Despite my frustrations, I could not help but be amused. I decided to play. In that moment, as I wrote on the soft square of tissue, careful not to rip it, the tension that had been fueled by frustration and injustice dissipated. I still wanted to convince her to let me go, but regardless of her decision, I felt that she had heard me. The push of the toilet paper signaled her willingness to continue to engage. I went to bed with a blanket of frustration, but the anger had left my body. My disappointment was about not being able to go to the event, not in my mother. This allowed me to not hate her the following morning.

While my mom did not name my feelings or hold me with understanding in her arms, she didn't completely disconnect. She delivered her solid decision that I was not allowed to go out with my friends that night, while still connecting with me and not trying to convince me to feel anything other than what I was feeling. In doing so, she created the opportunity for me to sit with my frustration, then move through it and come out the other side by tapping into my own resilience and recovery.

That feeling of being seen despite her not looking me in the eyes, and the feeling of being heard despite her not giving in to my imperative pleas, would not have happened had she not communicated with a cushion of humor. This experience instilled in me a playfulness and planted seeds for the satisfaction and desire I would later experience with my children.

* * *

Micah's many tantrums as a toddler gave me multiple opportunities to practice all that I had learned from yoga. I was often, but not always, able to enter that place of believing he was whole, accepting the as-is of the moment and recalling my ability to breathe and find patience just long enough to see how I wanted to proceed with the situation.

One early fall day, I arrived at Micah's preschool classroom to find that he'd had two bathroom accidents that day. He'd gone through his extra clothing and needed to wear a spare pair of pants the school kept on hand. Micah was in the bathroom with a teacher, resisting putting on the clean pair of pants, as they were not his own. His teacher, a patient woman, gave me a look that communicated the message, "Please take over here. My patience is running thin, and I have other kids to attend to at the moment."

I found a way to gently fit my body into an already full bathroom buzzing with several little half-naked bodies. I crouched down on my heels, getting close to Micah's level. He loudly declared, "I am not putting these pants on!"

I was acutely aware of the other parents coming to pick up their children and what they might be thinking. I was aware of the judgments from the teachers as he yelled and screamed about the clothing. I wondered what others in surrounding classrooms might be thinking as they listened to his shrieks. Part of me wanted to pick up his volatile body and shove his legs into the pants and simply carry him to the car. I knew he couldn't leave the school naked, even though the possibility crossed my mind. I got close to him, and as I looked into his eyes, I imagined he was feeling some level of shame and embarrassment. I felt for him and did not want to escalate the situation.

"I get that you don't want to put on somebody else's pants," I said. Knowing that calmness can be transferred from one person to another, I held him. I didn't tell him to stop or try to bribe him. I simply held him, and the more agitated he became, the calmer I became. I'd learned from practicing savasana, or corpse pose, the value of resting in stillness in order to incorporate all that my body and mind had just experienced. I'd also learned that when I slowed my breath down and brought my awareness to it, the body touching mine adapted to my slower speed.

This practice helped me to look beyond the exterior of this moment, beyond Micah's behavior and loud voice, to see that he was just having a hard time. After a while, he calmed down. The other kids returned to the classroom or left the building. I offered him our next step.

"Micah, you will get this toileting thing down. It's frustrating when you have an accident, but it's no big deal. We have to go home, and I know you don't want to wear your wet clothes. We need to leave wearing clothing, and if you put these pants on now and for the car ride, we can immediately change into your own clothes when we get home."

The redness of his cheeks from crying faded. He slowly lifted one leg at a time into the borrowed pants. Once we left the building, it was like he forgot he was wearing the pants at all. When he saw his friend on the playground with her mother, he asked if we could stay a bit and play. I knew this was exactly what he needed. What I didn't know was that this tantrum was about to change my life.

The mother of the child on the playground was one of only a few other mothers who did not work full time, so our midday pickups often aligned with one another. She had been watching the episode with Micah in the bathroom and had observed me with him on other occasions at the school as well. "Have you ever considered becoming a parent coach?" she asked.

"A parent coach? I didn't know such a thing existed."

"A parent coach," she explained, "helps parents find calm so that they can parent their children with greater patience and allow them to be who they were always meant to be."

My heartbeat quickened at this description. I had been thinking about my future career. I wanted to step away from caregiving and study something that would nourish my creativity. I had always loved photography and had started the application process for a full-time photography program. Midway through the application, I realized my naivete in believing I could do any kind of program full time. But the idea of being a parent coach intrigued me.

As soon as I had a few moments at home, I looked up parent coaching and saw that indeed it was a thing! After doing some research, I registered for a yearlong graduate-level program that would introduce me to a deeper understanding of child development, various parenting styles, and how each style has its own strengths and challenges. I would learn about ways to support parents in taking care of themselves so they can be the parent their child needs.

While I originally thought photography would be a great form of self-care, the path to working with other parents took me on a deep dive in which I uncovered more of my cultural conditioning. It nourished my self-care in ways I never imagined. Because of this, I have been able to help other parents see the beauty in their own children and find the joy in parenting.

CHAPTER EIGHT:
SOUL CARE

"You can't give to your children what you don't have yourself." This was perhaps one of the most profound messages I took away from Sonia Sumar's teachings. In other words, the more I cared for myself, the more I would have to give to my children.

My early understanding of self-care was that it was a form of escapism. It involved taking a break from my role of parent and caregiver. And while these breaks gave me time to reconnect to myself, they held no lasting effect. Later I would hear from other parents that self-care was something they knew was important but didn't believe they had the time to implement. That's where I was. Parenting a child with special needs could be all-consuming, and losing track of the self-care time was easy to do. I felt the tightness and rigidity in my parenting whenever my self-care suffered, but I also knew I needed to broaden my definition of self-care beyond escapism and exercise, which were not always available.

There is a level of self-care that goes far deeper than going to the gym, getting a pedicure, going out with friends or staying at a hotel room for a night. Don't get me wrong, these are all wonderful things, but they are just the tip of the iceberg. Caring for yourself is learning to be fully present and allowing yourself the space to feel your feelings. It is finding over and over again a place of forgiveness and gentleness toward yourself, as well as setting boundaries and honoring what you truly need in any given moment. This is where you can find the self-care you need most, the kind you can practice even in the midst of chaos. Filling your cup happens when you untether yourself from judgment. It happens when you slow down and connect with your breath so that you are able to see and hold yourself with compassion and understanding.

This level of self-care includes recognizing triggers. As parents, we often think our stress is being triggered by the behavior of our child, but our triggers exist inside of us. They come from an uncomfortable place within each of us, and what triggers one parent may not bother another. Instead of learning to acknowledge the source of that discomfort, we often learn to direct the discomfort away from ourselves in the form of blame and judgment. Mostly without even paying attention and just dumping judgment onto another person. In order to begin the untethering process, we have to remind ourselves to compassionately notice when we are in judgment.

Once you pay attention to the moments when you find yourself judging, you can slowly begin to pause there and acknowledge it. You might simply say to yourself, "Hmm. I am judging right now." Once you notice it, you can look behind the judgment and see what thoughts and beliefs you are holding about yourself or someone else. You can breathe. You can slow your breath and see where you feel judgment in your body. You can breathe into those places and see if you can soften. All of this prepares you to ask yourself what you would have to feel if you didn't judge yourself or that person.

At some point in my parent coaching training, I embraced the idea of finding self-care in the presence of my children. Kids invite us into these moments often in their early years. Mira's nightly invitations to her dance party—driving with music blasting and singing along—showed me the benefits of stepping into the interests and worlds of all my children. Whether you share the same interests with your children or not, when you drop into their world for a few minutes, it allows your outer "doing self" to melt away so you can connect with them. It's an invitation to see the world through their eyes and not through the lens of what they are accomplishing.

When I removed both Mira and myself from the ladder of accomplishment, I was much better equipped to connect with her where she was. I was much more easily able to be playful with the curveballs Micah threw at me when he pushed back against the tides of normality.

The fact that as parents we often feel compelled to fix our children, or somehow sense that our children are broken, comes from a societal and cultural belief that idealizes the "typical." It's this belief that puts parents on the treadmill of trying to make our children into something they were never intended to be. It keeps our focus on our children's behavior and achievements, rather than their soul and the unique life they bring to the world. I not only learn more about my children when I soften into their world rather than molding them into mine, but I learn more deeply about myself.

For each moment I have found myself triggered and agitated, I ultimately have learned that each and every trigger lives within me and can be connected directly back to a moment in my early years. The upset in wanting my child, even for just this moment, to be someone they are not is not about them at all. The upset is the messenger that is digging its claws into this moment, telling me to go within and see what belief I have been conditioned to hold.

Taking a moment to pause, to go within yourself and identify the trigger and what it is here to show you is exactly what fuels personal growth. This is inner self-care, enabling you to drop into curiosity and pull yourself back into the present moment. Step back from the thoughts in the future, the what-ifs and the fears and the "shoulds," and bring your heart and head to a place of neutrality, a place of what is.

* * *

I signed Micah up for swimming lessons at a place in town that had a great reputation. Learning to swim was nonnegotiable in my house, as it was for my parents.

"I know how to swim," Micah repeated over and over.

"I know you know how to swim, but you are not yet a strong enough swimmer that I can trust you alone in the water without supervision. You need to take lessons until you are good enough to swim on your own."

It was not lost on me that I, like my father, wanted my son to swim, and not only to swim but to be a stronger swimmer than myself.

I built in a solid hour to allow the potential tantrum from Micah between picking him up at a friend's house and the swimming lesson. As Micah placed his backpack down on the mudroom bench, I told him about the upcoming lesson. The predicted tantrum ensued.

"I am not going to the swimming lesson! I know how to swim!" he shouted.

I listened.

"I am not going to the lesson!"

My heartbeat quickened and heat rose in my entire body. My desire to control the situation and the fear that accompanied his insistence pulled up my own fear of the water, as well as my fear of what could happen if he didn't learn to swim. I took a deep breath and stepped into curiosity.

Sitting on the armrest of the chair where he sat, knees curled into his chest, I said, "You must have a really good reason for not wanting to go to this lesson. I would love to know what that is."

"I won't know anyone else in the class," he said.

Less than two minutes later, one leg released from his tight grip.

"I will know someone in the class. I'll be the oldest one in the class."

I realized he was afraid of standing out and being the worst swimmer. I could relate and understood.

"So you are concerned that you might know someone and that maybe you will be the oldest kid there. You also are afraid that you won't know anyone."

His eyes met mine and he nodded his head.

"I get that. I can't make you go in the water, but we are going to go to the lesson. How about if we just take a bag with your swimsuit and a towel, and you can see how you feel when we get there?"

He released his other knee and placed both feet on the floor.

Walking through the school's entryway, we passed paper cutouts of fish in every color glued to the walls, resembling a preschool classroom. I was aware that Micah, a current second grader, felt he was older than the population this school targeted. I introduced myself to the teacher and informed her that Micah might just observe. She was as friendly as could be and invited Micah to the pool. Armed with his tote bag, he sat in the chair refusing to budge.

My fears of him not learning to swim, my frustration of not being able to coerce him, and the reality of $200 lost kicked up an anxious breeze that pushed me toward annoyance and blame. I became angry at the school staff for refusing to give me a refund. I decided this swim school was not a great fit for Micah and we returned home, no wet swimsuit or towel to dry. I sat with myself, taking time to disconnect from my frustration about what had happened. I decided I would not give up on swim lessons for Micah; I simply needed to find a school that was a better fit.

The following evening, Micah announced he would take a swim lesson at the YMCA where he knew a friend was enrolled. I called and was able to get him into his friend's class. When the day arrived for the lesson, Micah came to the kitchen ready to go, his bag packed.

With a smile on my face, I asked, "Are we shopping again today or are you going to take a lesson?"

"I'm not sure," he replied.

I sighed. Honoring his willingness to go and admiring his ability to be in charge of himself, we drove to the Y. Together we sat on a bench alongside the pool as six other kids jumped into the water. I removed my jacket, then my sweater, as the room was warm and I realized I would not be joining the other parents observing from an area upstairs. With each layer of clothing removed, I set aside any expectation that Micah would go in the water.

I played out other scenarios in which he could learn to swim if this didn't work. There were private lessons. Perhaps he would be ready this summer. Whose agenda was it that he learn now? That was all mine. Here was an opportunity to be the parent to him that I needed years ago as a young girl when I submerged my body in the water, unable to speak up to my dad, disobeying my voice in order to please him.

"Mom, do you think I should go in the water now?" Micah asked 15 minutes into the lesson.

"I don't know. Do you think you are ready?" I asked.

With a solid yes, his fingers curled around the handles of his tote bag, he pushed the door open and went to change into his suit.

Micah spent about 10 minutes in the water that first class. I spent 10 minutes wondering if he would go in the next time. We discussed the lesson a bit in the car ride home. But what solidified my confidence in deciding to follow Micah's lead came as we held hands walking through the grocery store parking lot on our way to get a few things for dinner.

"Mom," he said. "I'm really proud of myself."

In taking care of myself, clarifying my concerns and noticing my fears, I was able to clean up my internal clutter so that I could be the parent my son needed me to be.

Years into my work and training as a parent coach, I continue to deepen my understanding of self-care, or as another brilliant mentor, Suzi Lula, called it, "soul care." The idea of soul care resonated so deeply within me. As I have learned and experienced, when our soul care is not occurring, stress, anxiety and resentment find a place within our nervous system and other parts of our body and make themselves at home.

An important piece of soul care involves embracing contradictions and holding love for your entire self—the peaceful and the rageful, the peacemaker and the bully, the accepter and the judge, the part that says you're enough and the part that tells you you're not. When you can embrace them all, you can have compassion for the voice that says you are anything but whole and know that you are. For me, soul care is getting back to a place of stillness where I can see far beyond the exterior, beyond the balance of my bank account, what art is on my wall and how many wrinkles I can count that day. It has helped me get to know myself, uncovering layer by layer the beliefs that clouded my inner belief over the years to reclaim the gifts my mother gave to me as a young child.

Today, I strive to give to every parent I work with the gift of seeing beyond our conditioning and the tight confines in which we live our lives in a truly unconscious way. I hope to help each parent find that place of grounding, their own unique warrior II pose where they feel firmly planted into the ground with surrender and ease. The place where play and curiosity infuse their daily life. This can all be found through soul-to-soul connection with their children, especially those children who are living in this world in a way we see as atypical. These differently abled kids are living from their hearts and souls in ways that the rest of us need to relax into and reclaim.

* * *

Sitting in my basement office in Newton, I listened to a woman in her 30s as she spoke about her inability to find calm with her 6-year-old child. The child was lagging in executive function skills. This mother was someone who grew up in a rigid environment. She thought every other mother had their act together and that she was the only one who couldn't get herself organized. Her inner critic flared each time she forgot where her car keys were or she was late getting her child to school. Her son often called her a "stupid mom," a "forgetful mom" or a "bad mommy." These statements stung because she believed them. I could completely relate to this woman. I had been that forgetful person, beating myself up for my ADD mind, which doesn't move in straight lines.

Her husband, who was sitting next to her, said that when he couldn't find the car keys because his wife had left them in her purse, it just wasn't a big deal. The keys always turned up. As someone who cared far less about how others viewed him, he accepted his wife completely. "This is part of who you have always been," he explained. "Why should I expect you to change?"

I asked my client to shift her perspective for a moment and imagine herself on top of a mountain looking down at herself as a mother. As she pulled back from a close-up on her life and viewed herself from this expanded view, she was able to see herself in her entirety—a person in the midst of her immediate family, her extended family, her community and the culture at large.

This mother saw herself struggling to navigate her constant self-criticism and self-judgment. She saw how these judgments were larger than life and how they had come to define her in some way. She saw herself moving through the world with the word "failure" flashing in neon just above her head. As her vision expanded to include other people, she began to see she was like many others who are just trying to get through the day, stumbling as they go. She saw all that she managed, together with the unconditional acceptance of her husband, friends and family.

I asked her what she would like to say to the mother she saw down below.

"Be gentler to yourself," she responded. "Of course you forget some things. This has always been you. Why do you expect that you should be someone other than who you are? Many of these things are not so important."

When you are able to look at yourself from that imaginary mountaintop, taking in the bigger picture of who you are, judgment tends to soften and dissipate, allowing space for compassion.

Alongside my development as a therapist and training as a parent coach, my yoga studies over the years have helped me arrive at a place of self-appreciation, where I am finally able to set my "stupid mommy" moments in a well of kindness. I've discovered that to bring my full and authentic self into the room with my clients, self-compassion is needed. Without the ability to feel empathy for myself, I would be ill-equipped to model such for others.

The beauty in this work is that I often learn about myself through my clients, just as they are learning about themselves through me. I too need to frequent this mountaintop when one of my children says or does something that stings. The pull toward taking things personally and self-criticism can be a powerful force. Pausing allows us to widen the lens, and widening the lens provides us with the view of our whole self, allowing the light of self-compassion to enter.

* * *

I am often intrigued that, after being away for a while, Mira's caregivers will say, "I need a dose of Mira." Mira has a way of connecting others to themselves. She finds humor in the things others often beat themselves up about. Can't figure out how to work the computer or the television? An adult might yell and curse. Mira laughs. Can't find your sunglasses or the car key? While an adult may enter self-judgment or blame someone else for moving them, Mira laughs.

Mira doesn't store her feelings deep within but instead expresses them and allows them to move on. She delights in her community, in connection with others, in playfulness, in food, and in music. These are all crucial elements for healthy development in children. She does not judge herself. She isn't cursed by the emotional chains of social media. She lives in the present moment all the time. The things that bring Mira joy are the same things that most of us need to reconnect to ourselves.

CHAPTER NINE:

TELLING TALES

When Mira turned 6, I began taking her on my frequent trips to Starbucks. Because she wanted to get out of her wheelchair in order to sit next to me, she always reached toward the tables with benches along the walls. I wanted her to practice the independent sitting skills she had been developing, so I would ask, "Mira, will you sit safely here while I get you some water?"

"Yes," she'd signal using her right hand.

"Show me how you are going to sit safely," I would prompt her. She would straighten her back and put both hands on the table. While I went up to the counter to get our beverages, I would leave her sitting alone on the bench.

For Mira, going to the coffee shop was about so much more than eating her favorite pumpkin bread. It was about getting out of the house, running into friends and neighbors, having some mommy-daughter time, and being a part of a community. As I waited in line to place my order, I would look over to watch Mira sitting unassisted at the table. I was filled with pride at her accomplishment and a sense of relief that, despite the messiness of our trajectory as we tried various therapies and yoga over the years, Mira had developed strength and core stability that had never been guaranteed. She had gained control over her body.

During one of our visits to Starbucks when Mira was a teenager, I looked around and considered our seating options. All the benches were taken. The only space available was one side of a table that was dedicated to wheelchairs. Three teenage girls, a year or two older than Mira, were sitting on the other side with their Frappuccinos and cell phones in hand. I debated whether to sit there and decided to forge ahead because there would be space for both of us to sit together on one side of the table.

"OK if we share this table with you?" I asked as I pushed Mira's wheelchair toward the table.

"Sure," one girl said.

The others glanced at Mira, then back to their cell phones, continuing their sporadic discussion between texts. I sensed their uncomfortable awareness of Mira and knew that by their age they probably would have internalized the social norm that it's not polite to stare or ask questions. I recognized their look of discomfort. I was always aware of the frequent glances toward Mira and noticed how others looked and then looked away when she drooled, screeched with joy or whined with unhappiness.

On this day, I tried to focus on Mira, wanting to fully enjoy our time together. But my thoughts about what these girls might be thinking diverted my attention. My awareness of the chewing noises Mira was making was greatly magnified. I immediately wiped away any bits of soaked pumpkin bread on her chin.

During another Starbucks visit, I was sitting with Mira and Micah when a family with two young girls and a baby boy sat at a table right next to us. The two girls, between the ages of 4 and 6, were engrossed in the intricacies of their frosted cookies. Just as they were about to eat the first bite, one girl and then the other noticed Mira. As Mira reached for the handle on her blue drinking cup, slowly and deliberately bringing the straw to her lips, the girls' gazes locked onto her. They stared gently without glancing at each other. The low hum of the coffee shop created a comforting background sound.

Until around age 6, children are comfortable around Mira. In contrast to the polite curiosity of the teen girls, the gaze of these younger girls was open and untainted by an ounce of discomfort. To them, Mira was simply a new kind of person. They were curious and wanted to make a connection, gaining an understanding of how Mira fit into their world.

Parenting Mira, I am constantly reminded that my expectations of how things "should" be can pull me into states of depletion, lack and fear. It's Mira's pure presence, her apparent obliviousness to potential judgment, that reminds me again and again to notice when the world of expectation pulls me to these places. Our coffee shop visits brought some unexpected lessons.

Dear teens at Starbucks,

We met recently at the long table by the window. I came over to ask if my daughter and I could join you and sit on the side of the table that you were not using. You took a quick glance at us, said yes and then turned your attention back to your phones.

As I wheeled Mira to the table, I was aware of your reactions, wondering if you would text each other messages discussing whether to stay or go. With each glance toward you, I was brought back to myself at your age, remembering my physical panic at the sight of a man I once saw having a seizure in the middle of a restaurant.

I have carried this fear for years, an aversion to any situation, person or place—like a hospital—where people's bodies seemed different or helpless. In certain circumstances, I've even felt a low level of nausea.

I told myself that sitting with Mira was a good experience for you, that it was important for you to see how some people differed from you in cognitive and physical ability. But in truth, I was carrying the weight of my own judgments, fearing that you would judge my daughter as a less valuable human being.

All the while, Mira was perfectly comfortable, enjoying her pumpkin bread and the warm atmosphere of the coffee shop.

She didn't care that she was wearing a bib or that some of the pumpkin bread missed her mouth and fell on the table. It was as if I needed to carry all the discomfort and insecurity I believed she should be feeling.

Your presence was a gift that day. You helped me to see how I create stories in my head—narratives that are not what Mira is experiencing and may not be part of your story either.

With gratitude,
A mother with a special needs daughter

* * *

As parents, the stories we tell ourselves can lead us into dark places where our shadows rise to the surface. Feeling threatened can trigger our worst fears of failure. When we allow ourselves to see what's happening, we can become aware of this so we can separate ourselves from what's really going on with our children.

I saw this clearly when a mother of five came to me for help because one of her children was struggling with depression. In the brief time we worked together, I could see how she and her husband loved their children and wanted the best for them. She had many stories of how the family enjoyed spending time together and how they loved to travel.

I listened as the couple told me about their kids, listing off their names, ages and aspects of their personalities. I began assembling the unique puzzle pieces that made up their family. Then the mother began listing all the reasons her daughter's depression didn't make sense: "She attends a great private school and gets excellent grades. She's the captain of her soccer team and has plenty of friends. She is beautiful and has so much going for her."

I could hear how difficult it was for her to understand that her child might be suffering despite being well provided for. She could check all the boxes she believed would make her daughter a happy individual. Yet the contents of these boxes, the beliefs and expectations handed down from family, culture and institutions like a synagogue or church, may have had nothing to do with who her daughter truly was or needed to become. Her husband nodded his head as she shared all they had done to provide a happy, wonderful childhood for their kids. I was almost certain that deep beneath their concern for their daughter was the underlying fear I had known so well, that somehow, despite doing so much for their kids, they hadn't been enough.

I focused on the mom, speaking from my heart as I asked questions about how they understood the daughter's problem and how they perceived her strengths. I wanted to know how they felt as parents, where and when they felt most connected to their child. I also wanted to understand how they were affected by their daughter's depression. I saw myself in this mother who was struggling to feel more competent by doing more and more for her children.

I asked her to share some of the ways she communicated to her children that they are accepted for who they are. I was expecting she would offer some fun stories that illustrated this family connection. Instead, the mother paused and pulled a Kleenex from the box.

"All they hear from me from morning until night is what they are doing wrong," she said through her tears.

She went on to say that her day always began with a mental script of how she thought the day should unfold: "I need to make sure the kids are up, tell them to make the bed, make sure they eat a healthy breakfast and tell them what nutritional source is missing from their plate. I need to remind them that the laundry they promised to fold and put away is still in the dryer, remind them of their after-school activities, make sure they've turned in their assignments and threaten to take away their phones if they can't put them down at the dinner table."

Any unscripted moments were a source of upset for her. Because she believed it was entirely up to her to make sure her kids completed everything on her running list—in short, to become their best selves as she envisioned—she was unable to make a true soul-to-soul connection with them.

My questions, as uncomfortable as they were, awakened an understanding that she had been following a script that wasn't working for her or her children. As I settled more deeply into the session, I was drawn away from my own script, the things I thought I was supposed to be asking. Instead, I allowed myself to be fully present. I trusted myself to sit with and hold space for whatever came up in the session.

Sometimes more scripted questions are worthy of asking, but when your kids don't give you the responses you think you should be getting, it may throw you into a tailspin and fuel some major power struggles—all before your kids have even left the house for school.

CHAPTER 10:

KINGS, SCULPTORS AND YOGIBOS

While living at home the year between college and graduate school, I responded to an ad seeking actors to join the Interact Theater Group in Minneapolis, Minnesota, a unique group of disabled and non-disabled actors. I don't recall spending much time deciding. It seemed like a good fit with my interest in pursuing a master's degree in drama therapy.

The sun had already set when I showed up the first evening and parked my car in the lot behind the dark-red brick building, which was home to this community of adults with disabilities. The building felt old and in disrepair, the air reminiscent of a hospital with a slight hint of mold. The furniture in the common areas had permanent dents from years of use. In this lobby, I met the company members, some of whom were residents and were accompanied by a staff member who seemed tired and a bit disheveled.

I spotted a woman who ended up being the director, walked up to her and introduced myself. She welcomed me, gave me a nametag and told me to make myself comfortable while everyone gathered. As I took a seat in a worn chair, I did my best to keep an open mind, even as I was slightly uneasy about the state of the building and uncertain about not knowing my role, what to expect or how to engage with the other actors. I thought about my moment of enthusiasm that led me to sign up for this group and held on to it, figuring I must have been there for a reason.

Inside a large open room with high ceilings and faded wood floors we began our first session. We started with introductions and then moved into some basic improvisational exercises. The group members were all curious about me, observing what I said and did closely. They even commented on the clothing I wore, but I felt no judgment behind it.

The director led us through standing body stretches, and as I reached my arms overhead, I felt my feet supported by the floor beneath me. Others in the group reached their arms in every other direction but over their head. The director did not redirect them but rather accepted each person's action and moved on. As the opening stretches and improvisation continued, I noticed my shoulders dropping, my jaw relaxing, my legs grounded but no longer tense. The parts of me that wanted to move became free to express themselves in the arena of play. I noticed I had no judgment of the others, and they apparently had no judgment of me. Whatever came out of my mouth or was expressed through my body found a simple acceptance.

As one person created a movement with sound, the rest of us repeated it. No one said, "I don't want to do that" or laughed at another. The greater the movement and sound, the more engaged everyone became. The more engaged we all became, the more the energy of playfulness and spirit filled the room. I noticed smiles and kindness in the eyes of the others as I allowed my movements to take up more space and my expressions to increase in volume. The more I engaged in our play, the more my thoughts about the space, the musty smell in the air, the knowledge that I was in a room with many adults with different abilities began to blur and fade. My initial awkwardness and self-criticism began to fall away. The simple game of tossing an imaginary ball to one another, paying close attention to whether it was a beach ball, a spitball, or something in between, and then catching the ball that was tossed to me lit up my imagination with an awareness of what was happening in the moment.

In the weeks that followed, I noticed how readily I left my discomfort and fear at the door as I entered the brick building. By the time I walked up the stairs to the lobby and auditorium, I was no longer in a room of adults with abilities and disabilities, but in a place where the most real version of myself was held in the safety created by this group of people, who on many levels seemed to be spared from the expectations, roles and judgments I held for myself.

This lightness and joy accompanied me home and served as a connector between me and my mother, who anxiously awaited my stories from the evening. Upon my return, I would describe the latest from our cast of characters. There was Joey, the 43-year-old man who always wore khakis with his belt half-fastened and a button-down shirt he habitually unbuttoned and buttoned during rehearsal. Then there was Claire, the older woman who never participated in our games but gleefully played the director's echo. Debra was the woman in her 20s who could rarely stand still, was constantly looking around and often interrupted others with nervous questions.

On these evenings, I rarely returned home from Interact Theater Group before 9:30 p.m., but Mom always greeted me with delight and then sat down on the stairs or the couch in the den anticipating a recap. After a few weeks, she began asking about the other members by name with a smile on her face and an occasional hand on her heart. No matter where she sat, her back was straight, and she gave me her full attention as I indulged her with my respectful impersonations of some of the residents. I could feel her absorbing every bit of the enjoyment and playfulness I brought to the room.

These moments of storytelling helped to revitalize the connection my mother and I had always shared through our love of theater, music, art and all things creative. The negative emotions I felt toward my mother—my fear of taking on her depression, of becoming her—were temporarily displaced by what I would later recognize as our soul-to-soul connection.

* * *

In 1995, I was fresh out of graduate school and the youngest extern in my supervision group at the Ackerman Institute in New York City. I had a good relationship with my supervisor and received feedback from both him and my peers, which helped me believe I was good at what I was doing. They responded positively to my creative work with drama therapy. While I loved the recognition of my artistic streak, I was often hesitant to dive deep into that current. Instead, I allowed myself to be swayed by the pull of the mainstream. Fearing judgment for getting something wrong, I contained my impulse to work more creatively with my clients. But soon situations began to crop up that invited me to incorporate these skills in my work more consistently.

David, a young man in his mid-20s, came to see me with his parents weekly. They were struggling with the fact that their son lived with them at a time when most people his age were living outside their parents' home and working. Short and stocky with a round face and black-rimmed glasses, David was developmentally delayed. He was high functioning, but he lacked the skills required to live on his own, find a job or navigate the world of stable relationships. Overall, he presented as someone much younger than his age.

Both parents understood David's limitations in the typical world and wanted help so that he could fit in. They needed to motivate him to get out of the house each day to a day program or a job. Without being aware of it, they wanted him to be someone he wasn't—someone he might not ever be.

His parents needed emotional support living a life they had not planned. Their other son had graduated high school with honors, gone on to college and law school, and was a few years into his first job at a law firm. They had known about David's special needs from the time he was 3 years old, but they had no way of knowing what it would mean to parent an adult child with special needs.

Within the first few sessions, all three of them became comfortable enough to show a bit more of their frustration and sadness. As the parents spoke about their feelings, David developed a slight slouch, his eyes looking away from his parents more often than not, his jovial disposition gradually disappearing behind a mask of shame and disappointment.

I sensed that while David's mom was tired and sad, she felt that taking care of him was her purpose. David's father seemed to be coming from a place of resentment that stemmed both from disappointed expectations and his feeling that having his son around the house all the time was taking its toll on his relationship with his wife.

When David's dad spoke to me, he looked directly at me. When David's mother spoke, she looked at me but regularly glanced over to her husband and David, keeping tabs on their emotional state with every sentence she spoke. I could feel this family's confidence in me as we sat in sessions. They were not wondering if I could help them, not questioning my youth or my lack of experience as a parent. They were there raw and ready to make a change, willing to hear any ideas or thoughts about how they could foster the connection between them and their son.

This sense of connection and acceptance allowed me to slip into a more improvisational mindset. I was able to step away from the traditional therapeutic approach and put some of my drama therapy tools into action.

David's parents often referred to him as the "son who thinks he is a king." They were expressing their feelings about making all his meals, cleaning up after him and driving him to various appointments, including the day program he attended when they could get him to go. As I sat across from them, unsure of where to take our discussion, I unconsciously slowed myself down. I let the image of a king sink in. With an exhale and not much thought, I asked David if he felt like a king.

"I would like to be a king," David said, eyes opening wide as he chuckled.

I got up from my chair and held my hands in front of me, palms curved around an imaginary crown. I walked a few steps over to David and asked if he would like to wear the crown. As I stood in front of him awaiting his response, I was momentarily struck by my fear of his parents' judgment. I suddenly saw myself as the 27-year-old therapist that I was, unmarried and with no children. Who was I to think I could help these people? As I felt my face flush with humiliation, David sat up straight, smiled, reached out for the crown and placed it on his head. The blood flowing back down into my body felt like a cool breeze on a hot summer day. I caught a slight smile from his parents and sat back down.

"If I were king," David proclaimed, "I would eat hamburgers every night. In the morning I would get out of bed, go to my job, and when I came home my parents would smile."

Tilting her head to the side, his mother grinned. A tear rolled down her cheek before she could wipe it away with her tissue.

"I would order my parents to go to a restaurant and a movie," David continued. I watched as his father's hand reached for his mother's.

I interjected, "What is the greatest thing about being king, David? What does it feel like for you?"

David sat up even straighter as his smile of delight turned to one of easy confidence. "Being king feels powerful and good. I can do anything I want because I am strong and people listen to me."

Over the next several sessions, we pulled out the crown when we needed to. Everyone, including David, was able to speak more freely about how he could have more of a voice. We discussed how his parents could take better care of themselves even if David continued to live at home. Whether he was king or not, we helped David identify his many strengths. He began to identify his king-like qualities even if he wasn't wearing a crown.

When they ended their sessions with me, I experienced a lightness. I had felt a greater authenticity and playfulness working with them, and these had been powerful tools for getting David to open up and his parents to see things from a different perspective.

Feeling excited and nervous, I shared my experience regarding David and his crown with my supervision group. I described the ease with which the idea came to me and the confidence I felt within myself as I allowed my creative energy to flow. I saw clearly that stepping out of the prescribed boxes of how I thought therapy should look, and letting those "shoulds" go, led me to a place of wholeness, where I was as real as I could be with my clients.

* * *

How do you connect with someone who can't express what they are feeling? What if they just aren't able to share by speaking up for themselves?

One of my favorite things to do when working with a new family was to ask the identified patient, the one the parents thought needed fixing and was causing the discord, to create a family sculpture. Bypassing talk therapy, which teenagers often don't respond to—and which in due course I would be asked to do with my own daughter—I'd ask the child to imagine their family members as clay that they could form. They were tasked with posing each family member to create sculptures that represented the way they saw them and to place themselves in the scene as well.

Alex, an 11-year-old, came in with his mother, father and two younger siblings. He wasn't participating in the discussion. As his parents kept asking him to talk, he sank further into the couch, curling up his body in a way that clearly communicated he was hoping to disappear. I asked his parents to hold their words and invited Alex to show me rather than tell me what was going on at home. Once his parents stopped speaking, he began to grin. He shifted forward on the couch and stood up in anticipation of shaping his siblings and parents into a form created by him.

Starting with his mother, Alex guided her to take a few steps so she faced a wall. He bent her left arm slightly and rotated her palm so that it was flat and facing up. He curved the fingers on her right hand as if she was holding something. He asked if he could use a chair and then silently directed his father to stand on it. He climbed onto another chair and pulled his father's chin down so that his mouth was open. He demonstrated how he wanted his father to raise his arm and point his finger at Alex.

Gazing at both his parents, Alex then considered where to put his two younger siblings. He placed his 8-year-old brother on the floor sitting in a cross-legged position with his arms in front of him as if he was playing with Legos or building something. He then led his 5-year-old sister to stand by their mom with her fingers clutching the hem of her dress.

Already, without having placed himself in this sculpture, ideas were presenting themselves regarding what role each member played in this family. His father stood larger than life, mouth open and finger pointed, while his mother looked away.

At this point, I wondered if the father, settling into his sculpted pose, was feeling the force of how he was seen by his son. As he held the pose, his body may have been bringing up feelings of frustration, which he had the opportunity to examine rather than simply feel and lash out or dump onto Alex through shame or judgment. I wondered if he could hold the pose long enough to see how his son positioned himself.

Next, Alex walked around his sculpture and sat on the floor, knees curled in, arms wrapped around his shins. He placed his head down, avoiding eye contact with anyone. Then he looked up and scooted forward a few feet, placing himself further away from the rest of his family.

Alex's parents were enlightened and humbled by the perspective Alex shared regarding his vision of the family. I led other families who came to see me through this sculpture activity as well. Once family members settled into their positions, I asked the child who did the sculpting if they were satisfied or if there were changes they wanted to make. I would then ask them to give each person a line to speak. If it proved to be too challenging, I'd ask, "If we put a plaque or a bumper sticker on this sculpture, what would it say?"

This openness and curiosity to find new ways of approaching issues has served me well as a therapist and as a parent of a differently abled child. Observation, reflection, and the willingness to ask questions from a sincere place of interest, not from a place of perfect formulation, have allowed me to make mistakes and to learn from my clients as they have learned through me. It is at the heart of an improvisational approach to both parenting and parent coaching.

* * *

Fourteen-year-old Emma sat across from her mother and looked at me long enough to make eye contact, grin halfheartedly and slump in the chair. She was probably thinking of 30 other places she would rather be than sitting with her family and a coach to discuss family dynamics. Her brother Sam, after all, was the reason they were here.

The parents' main concern was that Sam was not listening to them about things like getting off the screen or doing his homework. When asked, he'd make up stories and impulsively say something inappropriate. They also shared that when one of the kids was upset and angry, the whole family got thrown off balance and they all entered a space of yelling and power struggles.

The parents reached out to me wanting to understand how they could be more supportive of Sam, who was experiencing frequent outbursts, yelling, kicking and throwing things. Sam expressed remorse for his behavior and articulated that he wished he could act differently. I noticed he was tuned in to the session and extremely sensitive, frequently glancing at Emma for approval while fidgeting with some object under the table.

At one of our first in-home sessions, Sam requested that we sit in the Yogibo individual beanbag chairs that mold to your body. His parents, Megan and Ron, led the way to a room in the house where several Yogibos sat alongside other traditional chairs and a futon couch. I think Sam, whether consciously or unconsciously, wanted to create a less formal atmosphere for our session to minimize the feeling of a parent-child hierarchy.

Though I was familiar with Yogibos, Ron described a new way to position them so that it molded perfectly to my body, providing support to both my back and my arms. Settling in and feeling the support and flexibility as I adjusted my position, I set aside any inclination to fix this family's pain. I reminded myself that more than anything, I needed to be present for this family and to provide a safe, comfortable place for them to feel and communicate without judgment. I tuned in to my sense of being a solid, supportive presence and reaffirmed my intention to hold space for whatever feelings might arise.

Sam began our session by saying he didn't feel his parents trusted him.

"You have cameras watching me when I'm down here. You put so many restrictions on my screen time. How can I ever have a chance to show you that I can be trusted?" he asked.

Affirming Sam's statement, I responded, "So, with all these cameras down here and the restrictions on your screen time, it's really hard for you to believe that your parents trust you."

Megan and Ron became defensive, speaking about the number of times Sam had promised to turn the computer off after an hour but never did. Their conversation turned from trying to convince me that Sam couldn't be trusted to trying to convince him that these restrictions were necessary because time and again he had shown himself to be untrustworthy.

"So, yeah, we don't really trust him," they admitted.

"Would you be willing to consider what it's like for Sam to carry the weight of never feeling trusted?" I asked.

Megan and Ron agreed to try this. Exhaling, they relaxed into imagining what their son was feeling. I saw Sam shifting in his Yogibo with discomfort. When his parents looked at each other, I saw sadness and compassion in their eyes. Sam, teary-eyed, got up to leave the room. They both exhaled loudly, turning to me with questions in their eyes.

I offered a different perspective. "If we accept the idea that all kids want to do well, that they want to feel successful and worthy in the eyes of their parents, then it is our job as parents to figure out what is getting in their way."

"How are we supposed to get him to respect us and others and teach him resiliency if we don't address the behavior?"

Megan asked, tilting her head with skepticism but willing to listen to my response.

"I get that with some of Sam's behavior, like throwing things at the walls and slamming his hockey stick on the boards and toward the players, it is hard to commit to this belief."

Ron slumped into his beanbag chair and rolled his eyes.

"Entertain me for a moment with this idea. It is not our job as parents to fix our children's behavior. We actually can't fix the behavior. What we can do is get curious and understand what's going on underneath the behavior. The need that isn't being met or the skill that needs development is where we can do the work. If you continue to address the behavior by taking things away and punishing him, you are reinforcing the belief that he is a disappointment to you and that you can't handle his big emotions."

Sam needed clear limits and boundaries, but they needed to be set from a place of connection and empathy. He needed support from a place of neutrality, like the Yogibo, and without the knowledge of the past and the fear of the future getting in the way of what was happening in the moment.

I thought of the Yogibos that held us during our session, accepting our bodies in whatever form they landed. What if Sam's parents were able to consistently offer him a flexible but stable cushion of compassion so he could land more gracefully and regain a comfortable form?

As with all my clients, it is never about the child needing fixing. It is about parents becoming aware of the obstacles getting in their way of being the Yogibo, the container, solid enough and grounded enough to hold whatever lands on them, allowing the child to shape-shift, lean into and feel supported so that they can express emotionally, verbally or physically what is going on underneath the behavior.

CHAPTER 11:

HER BODY WILL DO

From the time she was 7 years old, whenever we practiced Mira's walking, her legs would cross, and one foot would often get caught behind the ankle of the other. I would stand behind her, stabilizing her lower body with my pelvis and thighs, using my hands and arms to hold her upper body in balance. She could do the stepping but kept getting stuck due to the turning in of her legs. There was no doubt that this would inhibit Mira from ever walking on her own.

When Mira was 9, her orthopedist began suggesting that she undergo a bi-femoral osteotomy, a surgery to correct the inward turn of both femur bones and to place a metal pin in her left foot to keep it from turning inward.

I had a strong visceral reaction to this suggestion—it felt so invasive, so permanent, so scary. I didn't like the idea of general anesthesia or surgery. Not being able to include Mira in the decision-making process, or explain it to her in a way she would understand, twisted my insides and left me feeling enveloped in a layer of nausea.

Each time we visited this doctor, I noticed my sense of guardedness. I believed that with every measurement of Mira's range of motion, and the doctor's recitation of the number of degrees to which she could move each limb, I was being graded. During the visits, the doctor would ask whether Mira was still participating in various alternative therapies. Though he listened and I didn't sense critique, I began to feel there was a competition between the traditional and alternative therapies we were doing.

I left the appointments with a feeling of failure and self-doubt about the various treatment modalities I had pursued for Mira. I was acutely aware of how easily I was drawn into a perspective of viewing Mira from the outside in.

When Mira turned 10, the orthopedist told us it was the best time for her to undergo the surgery. Her bones were still growing, and if we waited there would be a greater likelihood for more surgeries later. It made sense to me that having her legs and hips in proper alignment early on would allow the bones to continue to grow in alignment. I asked all the questions I could think to ask, trusting that he was the expert and fearful that if we didn't do it, we would regret it later.

During the weeks I was grappling with this decision, I went to Kripalu, a yoga, mindfulness and meditation retreat center in the Berkshires. I was there for a week to assist Sonia during one of her basic certification courses. Mira's upcoming surgery loomed large that week. As yoga and Sonia's teachings refreshed my soul, my body coiled and held tight to the knowledge of our decision. Parts of me felt like an imposter—I hadn't done as much yoga as I thought I would since the last training—and thoughts and feelings of shame and guilt around not doing or being enough for Mira dimmed the excitement and calmness of being there.

At the end of our first day, I sat in a large rocking chair facing a floor-to-ceiling window in the main building, taking in the winter vista of leafless trees outside. Sonia sat down next to me so we could review the day.

"Mira is going to need surgery on her legs," I said. "She's scheduled for an eight-hour bi-femoral osteotomy next month, and they are going to put a metal pin in her foot. I think I could have prevented this if I had been doing more yoga with her."

My fears of failing as Mira's mother constricted my throat and belly with guilt and shame. My heart raced, my face flushed and my entire body was in a cold sweat. How could I have stopped doing something I believed in? Yoga was going to be what kept Mira on the path to healing. Yoga was what I knew I needed more than anything else. Why did I not follow through? A tornado of questions swept through my mind. As my thoughts raced, Sonia's solid yet gentle grasp of my hands did not change.

"Cindy, my beloved," Sonia said. "Mira's body is just her body."

I inhaled deeply. I let out a long exhale. Was I expecting some sort of punishment or condescending lecture from Sonia, whom I knew to be one of the most nonjudgmental people in the world? "Her body will do what her body will do," Sonia continued. "The practice of yoga will influence this, but it won't have the ultimate say."

In that moment, something inside me shifted. I felt the shame and guilt lighten. A wave of understanding and forgiveness washed over me, carrying away the weight of those emotions. My body stopped sweating. My heart was no longer pounding frantically within my chest. Sonia leaned in to give me a hug. Her embrace held the same unconditional love and acceptance I first experienced with my mother. I realized how my sense of worth as Mira's mother was dependent on external validation from others. I was defining my success as a mother by the accomplishments of Mira, even though they were drastically different from the accomplishments of neurotypical children her age.

By the time I curled up in bed that evening, my definition of yoga had expanded. I realized the importance of continuing my yoga practice so I could allow Mira to unfold as she was meant to unfold and nurture her spirit above all else.

* * *

Over eight hours, Marc and I sat in the waiting area at Boston Children's Hospital while Mira underwent the surgery. Anxious to see Mira and nervous about her recovery, we held on to our hope about what the surgery could accomplish. Eventually the doctor came in to tell us that all went well.

What I didn't know and could never have anticipated was that Mira would lose a great deal of her independence after the surgery. Due to metal plates implanted at the top of her femur bones, she could no longer sit cross-legged on the floor— something she loved to do. Not being able to do this meant she could no longer push herself forward onto all fours and stand up on her knees. She could no longer dance unassisted, which she'd do while kneeling, bouncing up and down on her heels. During her recovery, it became clear that sitting back on her heels was quite painful for her.

This was possibly the beginning of a plethora of other complications with Mira's body and spine. Even after several months, when the pin was removed from her foot, she could only sit back on her heels a bit before wincing in pain.

When we discussed the pros and cons of surgery, the doctor had emphasized that Mira's standing and walking ability would improve, but he never mentioned the abilities she would lose. What if he had mentioned this when we discussed the possibility of surgery? Would we have made a different decision? I spent countless hours bouncing from being angry at the doctor for not being fully transparent with us to wondering if he even knew the potential complications to being disappointed in myself for not knowing what questions to ask.

Ultimately, I needed to have compassion for the part of me that believed we had made the best decision we could have made at the time. The surgery was done. I could not get back those hours of decision making. I couldn't rewind the tape to make a different decision and then fast forward to see the result years later. At some point, I realized that if I didn't reach a place of acceptance for the outcome of our decision and let go of some of my judgments, the energy I carried with me would be transferred to Mira through my interactions with her. Reflecting on Sonia's words at Kripalu just before Mira's surgery, I once again felt her energetic embrace loosening the tight grip of guilt and shame.

Over the years, I was slowly letting go of the idea that I should be all things to Mira—teacher, therapist, nutritionist, advocate and mother. I couldn't and didn't want to release myself from being her mother, but what I needed to examine was what I believed a mother—specifically a good enough mother—to be.

Mira's needs would continue to be many, but I would come to understand that my role as her mother was not to provide for everything. As I learned to tune in and look closely at what Mira actually wanted from me, I began to see the difference between what I believed I should do for her and what she needed. This is how I began to forgive myself.

CHAPTER 12:

GATEWAYS TO ENLIGHTENMENT

J oining a synagogue and exposing my children to Jewish education was not something I ever questioned. It was simply a nonnegotiable box to check as they grew up. I imagine this is similar to parents who attended church as children and had a positive association. It seems natural that their kids would also be involved with the church. Perhaps we only question our decisions and actions when there's a chasm between the assumed experience with the actual experience.

My experience as a child at our synagogue was a meaningful one. My siblings and I attended Sunday school every week from kindergarten through eighth grade and Hebrew school twice a week from fourth through seventh grade. Despite my occasional complaints, I enjoyed the carpool rides, getting out of the suburbs, purchasing candy from a nearby corner store and nurturing friendships with others who lived in towns other than my own. I became a good Hebrew reader, and as I got older, I took part in my synagogue's youth group. I established lifelong friendships with the kids I met there. While I may not have felt a connection to the liturgy or certain observances, the singing, the music, and the community with the other kids and families and rabbis touched me deeply. I felt a sense of belonging that held my entire family.

It was also a place that provided me opportunities to serve others, whether that was packing and delivering meals to those in need, performing in plays to entertain others, singing in the choir to bring joy to the elderly or babysitting younger children so their parents could attend services without interruption. I was given the opportunity to apply the values I was learning from my parents. My Judaism was the environment that allowed me to experience intention through ritual, intimacy through friendships, and connection to myself and my feelings through music.

Marc and I occasionally attended services at nearby synagogues in hopes of finding a place where we would feel comfortable as a family. One afternoon while paging through the local Jewish newspaper, I spotted an ad for a Jewish education program specifically for children with special needs. I called the number and left a message curious to hear a bit more.

Within a few weeks of that message, we received a call back from an organization called Gateways. We were invited to join a program they believed would be perfect for Mira. I felt a rush of excitement that someone wanted to include her in a program that could give her a Jewish education. Directly on the heels of my excitement came the thought that it would be one more thing to manage in our already busy world of therapies and appointments.

Nevertheless, I drove with Mira one Sunday to visit the Gateways class in a nearby town. The classroom was crowded with parents, children and staff members. Each of the dozen or so kids was accompanied by at least one parent, and they sat together at tables with various crafts, crayons, coloring sheets, and plastic letters and shapes for the children to hold and assemble. Some were engaged in art activities, while others were more interested in exploring the room.

A few of us were there to check out the program to see if it would give our children what they needed to receive a Jewish education. I looked around the room, taking in the behavior of the kids as well as the expressions on the parents' faces, which ranged from disappointment and despair to relief and wonderment. I felt an immediate longing to visit with the other parents, but it was clear that most of our children needed our full attention and were unable to engage in the activities without our guidance.

My nervous system settled when a song leader strummed her guitar strings, inviting us over with her melodic words. Parents sat on the floor or in pint-sized plastic chairs while the kids sat in their laps, on the floor or explored the room.

The song leader began playing "Hinei Ma Tov," "Here Is What Is Good," a song about the joy of community sitting together. The words and sounds instantly brought me back to my synagogue's classrooms, sanctuary and summer camp, where I sat in circles surrounded by friends, connected by song. I had learned this particular song in a variety of tunes, ranging from a playful upbeat call-and-response to a calmer and more soothing meditative sound. The music quickly transformed us from parents helping our children with projects in our own little silos to a community of unique individuals singing about how good it was that all of us, with all of our differences, were sitting there together.

I sat cross-legged and held Mira on my lap. Hand over hand, I assisted her in rolling her arms, clapping and patting her lap. She was bright-eyed and all smiles. I was excited that she was connecting with music and Judaism while getting her stretches in at the same time! I relished the idea of sharing something that had been so meaningful to me in my childhood. I felt hopeful that she might be able to experience her own community through music. It soothed my soul for a few precious moments.

When the song session ended, I looked around the circle and noticed some of the children were focused, while others were making awkward gestures as if they were uncomfortable or wanted to leave. Negative feelings began to creep up again. Suddenly I felt like a stranger, surrounded by kids and parents

I didn't know. A sense of connection returned as we went on to speak about joys and challenges of celebrating the upcoming holidays. I continued to vacillate between these moments of belonging and isolation throughout our visit.

* * *

Mira's and my first experience with Jewish special education ended up leaving me with a great deal of ambivalence. It was like wearing a pair of headphones with a different song playing in each ear. One ear heard a familiar melody to which I could relax. The other was flooded with discordant and off-key notes that made me uneasy.

While I felt somewhat connected to the other parents and their familiar expressions—a mixture of hope and defeat—an uncomfortable idea reverberated in me. Was this a consolation prize for those of us who couldn't succeed in the synagogue? What did that even mean? Succeed in a synagogue? It certainly wasn't a concept I had previously given a moment of thought to.

But I was also left with the impression that the program director and song leader were genuinely excited about the possibility of having Mira there. That they would provide Mira with a Jewish education and rituals and so much more. It was an opportunity for her to feel like she was a part of something larger than herself, a place where she could share her worth with others, not just her brothers and Marc and me. Her cousins, grandparents and other relatives would see she was fully able to take part and contribute in a meaningful way to our family and community. All my children would know they were worthy of receiving from, being a part of, and giving back to this Jewish community and the greater community.

For more than a decade, Mira ended up attending Sunday morning classes at Gateways for an hour and a half. She smiled each time Marc or I said, "It's a Gateways morning!" We had our own pre-Gateways ritual that included 30 minutes of enjoying tea and pumpkin bread at Starbucks before heading to class.

Each time we entered the glass doors of the Gateways building, we would scan a large board on an easel with each child's photo and name attached to it with Velcro. Grabbing the photo on her own was challenging, so I'd hand it to Mira, and she would hold it tightly until she reached the wicker basket where she deposited it to officially check in. I'd also hand her the photo of her teen volunteer, which she was to hold until we reached the classroom where she would hand it to the volunteer. I'd push her in her manual wheelchair, following the brightly colored line of tape on the carpet that led each child to their respective class. We'd often stop along the way as Mira casually dropped the volunteer's photo on the floor. When we arrived at her room, Mira's teacher and several volunteers always greeted her with a warm welcome, we'd chat a bit, and I'd leave her in their capable hands.

On Sunday mornings at Gateways, Mira would learn about the Jewish holidays, she would do art and music and enjoy snacks, and she became a part of the community. But it became so much more than Mira's Jewish education. I got to know several other parents at drop-off and would sometimes hang out and visit with them. Other times I went home, and Marc would go back and pick her up and visit with the parents. When Noah was in 10th grade, he became a teen volunteer there. For a teenager who loved his sleep, he effortlessly got out of bed every Sunday morning and put on his Gateways T-shirt to spend time with his student. Micah, who was years away from becoming a teen volunteer, became known for writing "future volunteer" on his nametag at Gateways events.

Every year for Purim, a spring holiday when kids and adults dress up in costume, Gateways, like many synagogues, held a carnival. Gateway's version was a welcome relief for families whose kids may have been completely overwhelmed by the sounds and stimulation at a typical carnival. There were games, food and prizes like at the other carnivals, but there were also extra volunteers who were very patient, as well as additional space like quiet rooms for kids who needed a break. Every person could be themselves at the Gateways carnival, without feeling isolated or like they were disrupting the event.

At Gateways, we felt a sense of belonging that was stronger than at the synagogue we joined a couple of years before Noah's bar mitzvah. Marc and I had every intention of getting to know the synagogue community and having a place that could hold our entire family. Everyone there was so warm and welcoming, including to Mira. But they did not have a program for her. The babysitters the synagogue offered for young children were not trained to care for Mira, who required one-on-one support. While they encouraged us to bring her to services, we never felt comfortable staying when she began vocalizing or whining. Perhaps if we had asked the synagogue to provide one-on-one support for Mira, it would have helped us, but it felt like too much of an ask to me. And even if I did ask and they obliged, I was afraid we would then feel committed to attend each week. I was conscious of and concerned about being "too much." On the days we went, we readied ourselves with Mira's cup and snacks, and we knew we might end up staying there for only 20 minutes or less, depending on her mood. It all just felt too tenuous. Eventually, we stopped going altogether.

As my insight into the true shape of Mira's Jewish education evolved, I realized once again it was not about fitting her into the mold of how things were done. It was about breaking the mold to reach the "neshama," or the soul of the education, ritual or life cycle event. From this perspective, instead of having unsatisfying conversations about all the things Mira wouldn't be able to do, my thoughts were flooded with all the possibilities there were to explore. I was learning to look at my child and ask myself, *What is her essence and how can I structure an appropriate environment around her?*

I had come a long way from my early years of parenting Mira when I believed it was my job to fix her, to bring her as close as possible to the "typical" I had envisioned prior to her birth. Yet there were still times when I found myself awash in waves of guilt and sadness, with my thoughts, judgments and criticism spinning me into a jumble until I was unable to catch my breath. At such times, I practiced holding myself with compassion, the ultimate soul care practice. Once I was finally able to move the judgment aside, that's when the creative space opened up. I would see what was happening and think, *Oh, there's that guilt feeling again.* And I learned to ask myself, *What is this moment here to teach me?*

CHAPTER 13:

COMING OF AGE

Congregants approached the main doors at the back of the sanctuary and spilled into the room. Some were dressed in khakis and button-down shirts or casual-chic apparel. Others were wearing suits or dresses. Some were attending a bat mitzvah for the first time. Others had participated in their share of these coming-of-age celebrations. I was certain most had not attended a bat mitzvah designed for a child with special needs. I imagine many wondered how my nonverbal daughter would read from the Torah. Or how she would participate in a ritual that had long been a primarily verbal experience.

As guests entered, they placed a kippah on top of their heads and dispersed among the seats. I stood in the sanctuary, hugging loved ones, surprised by the number of people who had carved time out of their day and traveled long distances to take part in the celebration. In addition to family and friends, we were joined by members of the temple who had read about Mira's bat mitzvah in the community announcements.

The ceremony of the bar or bat mitzvah is often seen as the pinnacle of the child's Jewish education, the culmination of many years of Hebrew and Sunday school. It is an opportunity for the child, now considered an adult in the Jewish community, to share their own interpretation of the Torah, to be a valued member of the community with something of their own to offer.

Scanning the room, my eyes landed on the empty seat that should have been filled by my mother. After years of undiagnosed chronic pain, and an inability or unwillingness to perform prescribed strength exercises, she had become bedridden. She struggled to sit up or walk on her own. My eyes shifted to where my brother and sister sat, and I felt the presence of our mom through each of us. I imagined the tilt of her head and the delight she would have expressed admiring the flowers that adorned the dinner table downstairs. I could picture her clapping her hands or tapping her legs along with the drumbeats, probably off by a count or two. I imagined her talking endlessly about the spirit of our synagogue and marveling at her granddaughter, whom she had never really gotten to know.

Mira sat facing the congregants with her teacher, Rebecca, on her right and our rabbi on her left. My mind drifted back to a meeting I'd had with the three of them and the director of Mira's program at Gateways to discuss our vision for Mira's ceremony. My heart was warmed by the openness and excitement of the rabbi as she spoke of hosting what would be the first special needs bat mitzvah at the synagogue. We discussed which prayers Mira would lead and the songs we would sing.

Mira used an iPad to communicate. I suggested that in addition to touching a symbol to initiate a prayer or blessing, symbols could be added to Mira's iPad so she could invite the congregation to sit or stand or join her in singing. This would give Mira the chance to truly feel like part of the community and lead us throughout the experience rather than just starting us off in prayer.

Sitting next to Marc, Noah and Micah, I tried to calm my mind. I started by focusing on the beautiful sight of Mira sitting tall in her pink wheelchair, her head adorned with the same purple and white swirled kippah as many of the congregants and a prayer shawl on her shoulders. I concentrated fully on taking in my daughter and her radiance. I did my best to stay in the moment.

Still, my heartbeat quickened with each racing thought. I recalled a similar feeling when I walked down the aisle at my wedding with Marc. On that day, my thoughts were so loud I couldn't hear the music of the quartet or the song my friend had composed specifically for that moment. Since I couldn't stop my thoughts now, I shut my eyes, closing the curtain to the external visual distractions around me. I connected with my breathing to bring myself into the present moment, using each breath to shift my focus inward, consciously inhaling deeply and exhaling slowly, calming my heart, centering my mind.

On this day, I wanted Mira's soul to sing, her essence to shine. I deeply hoped she was willing to participate. As I continued to center myself, I recognized that I had zero control over whether Mira would follow the program as rehearsed or opt out altogether. The day before, as we gathered in this same room for photographs, Mira wanted absolutely nothing to do with it. She cried and complained for nearly the entire hour. So while I hoped she would choose to follow the program now, I made peace with all possibilities. I accepted that the only thing I could control in this moment and on this day was how I chose to see her.

As the ceremony began, the love, acceptance, warmth and excitement in the room were palpable. Mira's excited gaze traveled from the congregants to her teacher, Rebecca, and then down to the iPad held in front of her. It was time for Mira to invite the congregation to rise and for her to lead a blessing. The room was silent. The iPad was a bit lower than the visual field where she saw best. Mira looked toward the screen. She lifted her right hand slowly, fingers rigid and splayed, and she touched the screen. The message directed all to stand. I let out a small sigh of relief. Perhaps things would go as planned.

Next, when it was time for a song, Mira touched the symbol

with the message that directed attendees to join her in singing "Mah Tovu," or "What Is Good." Though she was unable to verbalize her excitement with words, she squealed with joy. Her entire body vibrated—her way of dancing. I smiled broadly as I watched her. Everything was going well.

When the moment arrived for Mira to lead the congregation in the Shema—a central affirmation of Jewish prayer in many services—she touched the symbol on the left of her iPad screen that initiated the sound of Rebecca's recorded voice reciting the first part of the blessing: "Shema Yisrael, Adonai Eloheinu ..." To continue the prayer, Mira needed to touch the symbol on the right side of the screen to start the recording. She began to lift her hand and spread her fingers. But as her three middle fingers extended, she touched the symbol on the left, playing the first recording again.

Heat filled my cheeks.

The congregation was silent.

My heart pounded rapidly in my chest.

Rebecca gracefully held the iPad while the first part of the prayer repeated.

When the recording stopped, Rebecca placed the iPad first in Mira's line of vision and then moved it down a few inches. She patiently directed Mira to touch the symbol on the right. The Shema continued.

All was fine.

Mira was beaming.

She didn't care about the glitch. For her, it was just a moment of as-is.

The ceremony was not about showing everyone what Mira was capable of. It was about sharing the joy and meaning that Mira's Judaism brought to her. It was about giving them a peek into the window of Mira's journey through Sunday school and the bat mitzvah training she attended with other kids. It was about showing each person in the room who had come to celebrate and honor her that all of this mattered to Mira. Connecting to her faith and her community mattered. It was about showing the world that despite her physical and intellectual challenges, Mira had a soul that was luminous.

Like the prayer shawl that rested lightly on my shoulders that day, a sense of comfort wrapped itself around me. I let go of the fantasy of what I had envisioned for that day, for my child and for myself as her parent. I embraced the as-is.

EPILOGUE:
A LETTER TO MY YOUNGER SELF

Dear Cindy,

Your motherhood journey will not be as you envisioned. You will experience a level of fear and despair you have never known. You will feel it deeply—from the moment you go into labor with your daughter, with each update from the medical team before, during and after her birth, and with every second you spend by her side in the NICU.

You will shed more tears than you can ever imagine, so many private tears in the shower and the car. As each drop evaporates, so too will the fantasies you've been holding about mothering two children, mothering a daughter, mothering a typical child.

You will begin to reconcile these feelings as you connect to your inner voice and knowing. And as you bond with your precious girl, with her perfect rosebud lips and full head of hair, naturally streaked by some sort of internal sun. From those first moments you spend in Mira's presence in the NICU, a soul-to-soul connection will form with its own steady heartbeat. At times, it will be muffled by outside noise—the opinions and biases of the world around you. Many times, though, it will feel like a drum reverberating loudly through your entire body. You will learn to listen to it and feel it.

You will also learn how relative time really is. Nothing about your daughter, Mira, or mothering her will go according to the timelines prescribed by you or anyone else. At first, you will struggle with this. You will try every therapy under the sun to help her meet certain milestones. Your natural desire to help her reach her full potential will overshadow the fact that she is not meant to be measured by timelines. You will eventually realize it is not about who she will become, it's about who she is. She was born whole. She is a complete sovereign being exactly as she is.

You will reach many crossroads as Mira continues to grow and develop. There will be moments when you feel like you are not asking enough, not doing enough, not knowing enough. There will be times when you question your choices about procedures meant to help her live a more "normal" life. Hold yourself gently. You can never know what you don't know. Listen to your inner voice. Continue to remind yourself that she is whole and complete.

You will gain more from being Mira's mother than you imagined. Beyond what she teaches you about letting your intuition guide you and accepting yourself and others without judgment, you will come to understand that the most limiting *beliefs are often self-imposed. Mira will show you how to accept the as-is, to embrace the freefall. And it will allow you to truly live in the moment and experience great joy, the kind your beautiful girl radiates naturally from the inside out.*

With love and compassion,
Cindy

ACKNOWLEDGMENTS

I am in deep gratitude to Dr. Shefali Tsabary, who encouraged me to write this book. She helped me deconstruct the belief that I am not a writer and move toward the understanding that I have an important story to tell. And that by not writing this book, I would be denying others the opportunity to learn from my experience.

I honor the patience and commitment of Dara Lurie, my writing coach, who not only nourished my development as a writer but was always one step ahead of me, knowing the exact questions to ask in order to access my material, even if it was one paragraph at a time.

Endless thanks to Tova Mirvis and Elizabeth Marglin for their willingness to read multiple drafts, offer ideas to move me through my writer's block, and give me multiple opportunities to practice being vulnerable, all while offering encouragement along the way.

To Suzi Lula, whose gift of teaching self-compassion and soul care, along with the support of my Permission to Thrive family, helped me write this book more than they will ever know. This book could not have happened at any other moment.

To Sonia Sumar, whose wisdom continues to ripple with each downward dog I practice. I am eternally grateful to have walked into her yoga studio.

Searching for publishers, I couldn't be happier than to have landed with Publish Her. Chris Olsen and Heidi Parton and the team embraced this book, and their dedication and input cradled me with support and kindness.

To so many family members and friends who have opened their ears and hearts for numerous years, listening to and supporting me in this process.

To Marc, Noah, Mira and Micah, who continue to be my greatest teachers. I am beyond blessed to call you my family.

ABOUT THE AUTHOR

A certified Conscious Parenting Coach, trained yoga practitioner for children with special needs, and former family therapist, Cindy Kaplan has dedicated her career to helping individuals and families communicate, connect and grow. Twenty years ago, after her daughter suffered a brain injury at birth and was diagnosed with cerebral palsy, Cindy realized the cultural constraints parents often blindly follow. Over time, and with the practice of yoga, she discovered that parenting from a centered place enables parents to interact in ways that simultaneously support their own personal growth and the development of their children. Today, she guides parents in finding compassion, confidence and joy through her coaching practice and community.

Cindy lives in Newton, Massachusetts, with her daughter, Mira, youngest son, Micah, two dogs, and her husband, Marc Weisskopf, a professor at the Harvard School of Public Health. Her adult son, Noah, lives in Boston.

Made in the USA
Monee, IL
01 September 2022